Strategic Leadership for a Change

Strategic Leadership for a Change

Facing Our Losses, Finding Our Future

KENNETH J. MCFAYDEN

THE
ALBAN
INSTITUTE
Herndon, Virginia
www.alban.org

The Alban Institute
2121 Cooperative Way, Suite 100
Herndon, VA 20171

Cover design by Spark Design.

Library of Congress Cataloging-in-Publication Data

McFayden, Kenneth J.
  Strategic leadership for a change : facing our losses, finding our future / Kenneth J. McFayden.
     p. cm.
  Includes bibliographical references.
  ISBN 978-1-56699-392-0
  1. Christian leadership. I. Title.
  BV652.1.M34 2009
  253--dc22
                                    2009022012

09   10   11   12   13   VP   5   4   3   2   1

Contents

Foreword

Everyone talks about the importance of leadership these days. In the business, nonprofit, educational, and religious worlds it's no longer management that matters; it's leadership. This interest has spawned an array of books about leadership. Taken together they offer complex, usually confusing, and often contradictory pictures of what it means to be a leader. There are, for example, "no easy answers," and yet there are "twenty-one irrefutable laws" and coincidentally "twenty-one indispensable qualities" for leadership. To meet the leadership challenge one must be a transformative servant with visionary power, executive charisma, and a nonanxious presence. One must have the skill of a jazz musician to manage a team of rivals, create reality, lead deep change, manage conflict, deal with strategic planning, and provide faith resources that help people make meaning in their lives, while at the same time caring for one's own personal, spiritual, and family life. There's servant leadership and spiritual leadership, primal leadership and principle-centered leadership, organic leadership and intuitive leadership, courageous leadership and resonant leadership, humble leadership and moral leadership. One can read about and learn from the leadership practices of Abraham Lincoln, Paul, Lao Tzu,

Walt Disney, Colin Powell, Robert E. Lee, Eleanor Roosevelt, Billy Graham, Santa Claus, and Attila the Hun. Leadership has been compared to killing cockroaches, walking naked into the wilderness, playing golf, and being like Jesus.

Even with all of this there seems to be a significant lack of leadership—at least the kind of leadership that makes a difference in today's world. In the church, pastors and other leaders struggle to understand their role and to develop the skills that are needed to play that role effectively. Those who try to keep up with all the newest writing, the latest techniques, and the most recent strategies have learned that this is a futile effort. None of us can ever know everything there is to know about leadership. None of us can even hope to know all that it would be good to know. We're forced to pick and choose—to read a limited number of books and develop expertise in a limited number of skills. We have a responsibility to do that. We also have a responsibility at some point to let go of the pursuit and simply trust who we are, what we know, and the power of God at work in our midst.

One way to focus our efforts is to think about leadership from the perspective of change. All leadership these days is about change. Both people and institutions need to change if they are to survive, let alone remain vital, in today's rapidly and radically changing world. This is a challenge for every organization, but especially so for the church, for we have a special, even sacred, charge to maintain a tradition. We cannot let go of the past lightly. We need to be clear about the nonnegotiables when it comes to change. And yet we also need to be willing to let go of much, knowing that the Spirit is at work among us, bringing something new into being. This is where the problem often occurs—sorting out the wheat from the chaff, the package from the wrapping, the traditions of the faith from the customs of the congregation. It takes highly skilled leaders to bring a congregation through this process, for it inevitably means disagreement and often means conflict. And in the end it will mean loss for at least some of those involved.

It is for this reason that the book you now hold in your hands is a necessary and helpful contribution to the literature on congregational change. Most books about leading change focus on the vision—what will be. This is important, for the vision is a great motivator, providing a common goal for which to strive, a picture of an end result that makes the struggle worth it. This book recognizes the importance of vision and talks about its power to enable change. Few books, however, deal significantly with loss. This one does, and for that we should be grateful, for in doing so it gives us insight into ways to overcome what might well be one of the greatest obstacles to effective and faithful change in the congregation.

It's often said that people fear change. However, it's not change we fear so much as loss. If we don't talk about the loss we can never move beyond the fear, so the fear blocks us. Fear becomes the obstacle to change. If we don't talk about the loss we may never discover that what we feared we would lose may not be lost at all. Unfounded fear becomes the obstacle to change. This book helps us deal with this reality, because it quite rightly recognizes the need to work through feelings related to both real and imagined loss in order for change to happen.

Drawing on the resources and insights of others, as well as his own experience as a chaplain, pastor, and educator, Kenneth McFayden explores the loss that is always experienced in the midst of change. He then offers ways in which leaders can help members of their congregations engage the discussion in order to sort out real from imagined loss and then deal with the reality. Facing the pain of loss is not easy, but it is essential for both individuals and congregations who understand the need to change in order to be faithful.

It's only after helping us understand the need to face the pain of loss that Ken McFayden turns to the important role of vision. And here also he offers something important to all those who seek to lead change. Vision for him is not just a statement crafted by a committee (with the proper input of the entire congregation, of course) in order to be pithy, pious, and profound. It is rather a vision grounded in the reality of values and stories—a vision rooted in the living and remembering of the congregation. This is the only kind of vision that has the power to sustain the members of a congregation in the midst of change, for it is one that lives in their hearts and is an expression of their faith. It is also one that is broadly affirmed.

The challenge leaders face today is a great one. It is nothing less than translating the Good New of Jesus Christ into the "language" of today, of making it relevant to a culture that is vastly different from the one that shaped the church that thrived during modernity and Christendom. All of us, at one time or another—sometimes more often than not—feel inadequate to that challenge. If the challenge is great, so is the potential. In more and more congregations that potential is beginning to be realized. They are congregations that have faced the need for change, endured the loss that is involved, and embraced a vision for the future. In doing so they have been able to carry with them much from their past that is to be cherished. Resources such as this book are a vital part of this ambitious process. They do not offer a blueprint but rather a way of seeing and understanding that enables us to honor the past experiences of those we lead even as we move together into the future that God has in store for us and for the church.

Jeffrey D. Jones
Author of *Heart, Mind, and Strength: Theory and Practice for Congregational Leadership*

Preface

I feel as though I have been working on this book for eighteen years.

In a master of theology degree program in 1990 and 1991, I wrote a thesis, *The Implications of John Bowlby's Theory of Separation Anxiety for Pastoral Care with Hospitalized Children.* In this research I came to appreciate Bowlby's examination of the relationships among attachment, separation, loss, and mourning. My thesis linked this research to my experience in clinical pastoral education at Kosair Children's Hospital in Louisville, Kentucky, where I was assigned to the burn unit. Children on the unit, isolated from their families because of the risk of infection, suffered acute separation anxiety.

After finishing the master's degree and earning a doctorate of philosophy, I found the relationships among attachment, separation, loss, and mourning helpful in a ministry development center, where I worked for six years with seminarians, pastors, and other church leaders on call discernment, vocational development, effective leadership, boundary management, burnout, and conflict management. In that setting, I consulted with congregations and judicatories on team development, conflict management, and strategic planning.

As a faculty member at Union Theological Seminary and Presbyterian School of Christian Education in Richmond, Virginia, I have developed courses in religious leadership that build on my academic background in pastoral care and counseling, my training in clinical pastoral education, and my experience in the ministry development center. Over time, I have refined the concepts in this book for congregational leaders.

When I began a sabbatical leave in the summer of 2007, I planned to write a book on "Leading in the Face of Loss." I had spoken on this topic in a variety of contexts and had been encouraged to publish a resource for church leaders. Late that summer I became aware of another book on this topic: *When Steeples Cry: Leading Congregations through Loss and Change*, by Jaco Hamman. When I compared his emphases with mine, I saw that my own book needed to have a focus somewhat different from the one I had envisioned. I spent a year refining my ideas and deepening my perspectives on the dynamics of attaching anew, the relation of vision to change, and the discovery of vision in values and stories.

Audience

This book is for congregational leaders. Pastors, other staff members, and lay leaders face significant opportunities and challenges as congregations face change, experience loss, ponder their future, and yearn for leadership. I have sought to write in a style that will invite such readers into conversation. My intent is to make substantial scholarship accessible to congregational leaders without overwhelming them.

Second, this book is for church governing boards. It seeks to guide congregational boards in responding to opportunities and challenges, and it offers perspectives for regional and national judicatory leaders who work with congregations to discover new possibilities amid change, loss, and grief.

Third, this book is for seminarians. It is a resource for courses in practical theology, congregational studies, and religious leadership. I hope it will increase the effectiveness of future leaders.

Finally, this book is for other leadership theorists. I hope my perspectives will stimulate theirs and advance conversations. My perspective is based on my identity, experiences, and values. Other theorists' insights will broaden and deepen the capacities of congregations and leaders for faithful and effective ministry in a time of change.

As I think of these diverse audiences, I am mindful of ongoing conversations about whether leaders are born or made. My assumption is that leadership is *learned*. Whatever gifts people bring to the functions of leadership, they must learn to be leaders. They must understand a context and create healthy relationships with followers and other leaders. I hope that this book will advance the learning of individuals and groups as their congregations engage in ministry.

With Gratitude

A book that evolves over eighteen years benefits from many relationships that have offered insight, encouragement, and support. I am grateful to G. Wade Rowatt, the professor who introduced me to the work of John Bowlby and supervised my thesis, and to the clinical supervisors who sharpened my perspectives as I integrated theories and practices of ministry.

I appreciate all that I have learned about change, loss, vision, and leadership from pastors and other church leaders, congregations, seminary students, and faculty colleagues. As I listen to their experiences and insights, I continue to learn.

I am grateful to the board of trustees of Union–PSCE for a sabbatical leave to focus my energies on this book. Many thanks to the president of our seminary, Brian K. Blount, and to the academic dean of our Richmond campus, John T.

Carroll, for their encouragement as I have worked toward its completion.

My thanks go also to the publishing team at the Alban Institute for many expressions of support for this book. When I presented my idea to Richard Bass, he responded with enthusiasm and offered hope for publication. Editor Beth Gaede has invested much in each page. She is a writer's dream—instrumental in making this material more clear and accessible to readers—and a reader's dream as well.

I am grateful to members of my family. I am blessed by loving and healthy relationships and appreciate how each one has helped me to become a better person.

Most of all, I am indebted to my wife, Narola. She is the person with whom I have learned the most about *attaching anew* and the hope that points toward a bright future. I dedicate this book to her.

Introduction

My goal was to get a job as a waiter in a nice restaurant—satisfying customers, working hard, receiving generous tips. I could only imagine the ways I might spend the discretionary income I would earn in a part-time job.

It was August 1979, and I was a college sophomore. In search of a job, I visited all the fine restaurants within walking distance of the campus, hoping my application to wait on tables would be accepted. At one restaurant, an upscale steak house, the owner responded that he did not hire waiters, only waitresses, but that he needed an assistant manager. His assistant manager had fallen off the roof while working on his house, breaking a leg; he would be unable to work for a few months. When I asked about the job responsibilities, the owner said, "Everything except for owning the restaurant and waiting on tables." I liked this man, accepted the job, and began my new position within the week.

For the next three years, I spent many hours in that restaurant and loved the work. As a sophomore, I worked full time while taking a full course load. As a junior, I reduced my work hours to twenty-five a week. As a senior, I cut back again, to twenty hours.

I spent a lot of time in that restaurant. I ate well and inexpensively. I learned the importance of working graciously with people and developed leadership and management skills that complemented my undergraduate studies as an economics major. I learned to cut steaks to the ounce at customers' tables and to grill those steaks to perfection. I learned about cash flow and inventory control. I learned to interview and hire applicants, to supervise employees, and even to terminate them. As I progressed through my studies, I struggled with whether to pursue a career in the restaurant business or to respond to an emerging call to pastoral ministry and to enroll in seminary after finishing college.

The owner of the restaurant, who was like a second father to me, was aware of both my love for the restaurant business and my movement toward pastoral ministry. In the spring of 1981, I had resolved my vocational struggle and decided to go to seminary and train to serve as a pastor. My employer was less resolved. One day that spring, he walked over, put his hand on my shoulder, and said, "Ken, you have a lot of potential in the restaurant business. I know you are thinking about going to seminary and becoming a pastor. I don't know if you've made a final decision. If you will come to work with me in the restaurant business, I will buy a restaurant for us and give you half the ownership the day you begin."

I'll admit that his offer was tempting. The restaurant was worth from $750,000 to $1 million at the time. I responded, "I appreciate your offer, but I have decided to go to seminary, to become a pastor, and to serve in a congregation."

The owner didn't miss a beat, and I could see the wheels turning in his head: "Heck, man, I'll buy you a church. Think of all the money we can make. We can hit 'em twice—you pass the plate in the worship service, and we'll serve lunch afterward and hit 'em again."

He was kidding—I think. Can you imagine what such a church might look like? It would probably be known as The Church of the Profits. People would keep coming back as long as they were well fed, as long as the menu matched their appetites, as long as they were served promptly (and not inconvenienced if others were served first), and as long as the prices were affordable.

Perhaps this scenario reflects the model of leadership that many congregations want—and expect:

+ Leaders accurately assess and respond to the appetites of those who make their way to the table.
+ To make the church more attractive, leaders suggest that a life of faith is easy, perhaps even effortless.
+ Leaders point toward the bliss of transformation in Jesus Christ without identifying the costs of discipleship at the heart of transformation.

A Hypothesis and a Purpose

This book builds upon a simple hypothesis: the church both yearns for and resists effective leadership, particularly trans-formational leadership. This hypothesis points toward the difficulties congregations and leaders face as they sort through conflicting messages in times of change and as they seek to respond to opportunities, challenges, and choices. Congrega-tional leaders may feel immobilized, caught in a double bind, without a clue as to how to escape it. This book seeks to pro-vide insight for congregational leaders who find that others both yearn for and resist their leadership.

Many congregations see significant change both within and beyond their walls. Members and leaders may experi-ence a permeating sense of loss. The intensity of their grief is shaped profoundly by the degree of attachment they have felt to what has been lost, or to what they fear losing. People also feel varying degrees of attachment to a congregation's iden-tity and ministry. Relationships and activities that are vital for some are peripheral to others.

Amid change, loss, and grief, congregations yearn for lead-ership, though members' expectations differ as to what con-stitutes effective leadership in response to their needs, hopes, and priorities. Some want leaders to guide them through fairly complex change. Others want leaders to recapture elements of the past that have been diminished or lost over time. Still others want leaders to bring about reconciliation among groups in the congregation that are competing for limited resources. Some want leaders who are not bound to tradition and who offer fresh approaches that will yield a bold vision for the future. Some want leaders who will establish priorities for the appropriate allocation of resources. And many want leaders to help them avoid the pain of change.

In a time of change, loss, and grief, congregations resist leadership. After all, leadership requires a response by those who follow that is born of hope and based on trust. Leadership assumes that those who follow will be open to more change and willing to work hard toward new realities. People yearn for leadership for various reasons. A leader deemed effective by some is seen as ineffective by others. Many congregations cannot bear such a split in how leaders are viewed, as if divergent perspectives on the effectiveness of leaders might destroy congregational cohesion and unity.

A complex bind results when congregations both want and do not want leadership. This double bind incapacitates leaders who do not know how to respond to the congregation's opportunities, challenges, and choices, and do not know how to lead people who are confused about what constitutes effective leadership.

The purpose of this book is to provide congregational leaders with new insights and tools for exercising strategic leadership, viewed here as

- ♦ Appreciating the interrelationships among change, attachment, loss, and grief.
- ♦ Assisting the congregation in naming and understanding actual and anticipated losses, differing levels of attachment by individuals and groups within the congregation, and expressions of grief.

+ Guiding the process of grieving to enable the congregation
  to accept the reality of its loss and to attach anew.
+ Comprehending the centrality of a vision for the future as
  the congregation increases its capacity to attach anew, and
  understanding the role of vision as a bridge between past
  and future.
+ Demonstrating the capacity to reflect theologically as the
  congregation moves through change, loss, grief, and the
  work of attaching anew, and as it aligns its vision with
  God's vision and understands processes of change as processes of fulfillment.

Key Sources for the Book

Multiple sources inform the content of this book. In the
field of attachment theory, I give primary attention to the
work of British psychiatrist and psychoanalyst John Bowlby
(1907–1990), who is considered the father of attachment
theory. Bowlby provides significant frameworks for understanding attachment, loss, and grief; the powerful dynamics of separation anxiety in the face of anticipatory loss; and
the importance of a reliable base of security for healthy human development. Supplementing his perspectives are the
contemporary works of psychologists Peter Fonagy, Robert
Karen, Mary Main, and David Wallin, as well as Lee Kirkpatrick, who has examined attachment in relation to the psychology of religious experience.

   In leadership theory, Ronald Heifetz provides profound
insight on the crisis of leadership and the art of leading in
adaptive change. John Kotter articulates key perspectives on
the processes of change and the place of urgency in enabling
openness to change. Nancy Barger and Linda Kirby consider
the challenge of change in organizational life, particularly
for those who make and implement decisions. Richard Morrill examines strategic leadership in relation to narrative and
vision.

In exploring dynamics of leadership in congregational life, Gilbert Rendle offers perspectives on and tools for leading change. Jaco Hamman considers leadership in relation to loss, and the role of leaders in helping congregations mourn. Gilbert Rendle and Alice Mann explore leadership in relation to strategic planning as a practice of discernment.

Biblical and theological perspectives that inform this book and enhance its relevance to congregational life and leadership start with the principle that leadership is an expression of discipleship. Church leaders first are followers, always responsive to God's call, presence, and empowerment through the Spirit. For us as followers, the call to follow sometimes requires a change in our defining points (Gen. 12:1–4; Mark 1:16–20). This change may be painful as we experience a profound sense of loss. Yet we grieve our losses with hope (1 Thess. 4:13) as we discern change in relation to the fulfillment of God's purposes.

Two sets of experience provide important sources of information. I bring more than a decade of case material from my work with pastors, staff members, church officers, church members, and congregations. My experiences with individuals and groups have informed the ways I interpret the sources mentioned above.

You bring experiences to this book that will stimulate engagement with my perspectives and make the book your own. Your engagement will enrich the material as you assess which components are most relevant to your context. Each chapter offers reflective questions to stimulate thought, discussion, and application.

For Reflection and Discussion

1. How is your congregation changing?
2. In the midst of change, what signs do you see of a yearning for leadership?
3. What expressions do you see of a resistance to leadership?

CHAPTER ONE

The Call to Follow, the Call to Change

Now the Lord said to Abram, "Go from your country and your kindred and your father's house to the land that I will show you. I will make of you a great nation, and I will bless you, and make your name great, so that you will be a blessing. I will bless those who bless you, and the one who curses you I will curse; and in you all the families of the earth shall be blessed." So Abram went, as the Lord had told him; and Lot went with him.

GENESIS 12:1–4A

The call to follow is a call to change.

In this powerful story of call, God calls Abram to *go from*, to leave behind much that has defined him—to go from his country, his kindred, and his father's house. In other words, God's command is a call for Abram to leave behind significant dimensions of his identity, defining points with deep roots in relation to his immediate family, his extended family, and his sociocultural identity. It is a call for Abram to embrace God as his primary and ultimate defining point, trusting God to lead him into a largely undefined and ambiguous future.

The depth of Abram's faith inspires me. His willingness to leave so much behind, without a clear sense of his destination, amazes. Abram, with Sarai and Lot, exhibits extraordinary confidence in the promises of God and responds in faith. If such a call came to me, I fear that my reaction would be one of ambivalence—a desire to go from, to be faithful to God, but also a yearning for the details of where I would be going. Perhaps this reaction reflects my need for predictability. Perhaps my response to a call to follow, and a call to change, would reflect my desire to minimize risk, to guarantee a positive outcome, and to maintain a semblance of normality, order, and control.

Perhaps many people of faith would experience such ambivalence.

Maybe I would respond as Abram did if God provided more detail of what my following would entail. Ideally, God would provide a map identifying the destination and possible detours to avoid a blocked road; a map that would allow me to calculate the costs of the journey and to assess the cost-benefit ratio of following; a map by which I would navigate my own way, trusting myself and my map-reading skills.

God provides no detailed map to Abram, just as God provides no detailed map to us. Rather, God leads the way, calling Abram and us to trust God and to embrace God as our ultimate defining point. God is our certainty amid change and the uncertainty it brings. Our response to God's call to follow demonstrates our openness to change, even when we must leave significant dimensions of our identities behind; it allows us to grow in faith during the journey ahead.

A Desire to Grow

We want to grow. On many occasions, I have heard these words from members and leaders of congregations who are keenly aware of a loss of members over the past few or the past forty years. These members and leaders yearn to fill the pews and realize that the smaller the congregation becomes, the emptier the sanctuary seems. Less money is dropped into the offering plates; the pool of volunteers shrinks, as fewer members are left to serve on committees, to teach Sunday school classes, to bring food for church dinners, to lead youth groups, and to sing in the choir. Each of these variables is a poignant reminder that if church membership does not grow, the congregation will surely die.

We want to grow. These words echoed through a church leadership retreat I led several years ago—a retreat whose agenda was to refine mission and vision statements and to construct a strategic plan. The impetus behind the plan was simple: a congregation's desire to grow.

During the twenty-four-hour retreat, I heard the refrain "We want to grow" many times—from longtime members of the congregation and from relative newcomers. Clearly, their motive for growth was to fill the sanctuary, to boost participation in Christian education classes, to offer more programs for all ages, and to increase the size of the small staff. Their building was sufficient to allow for such growth. What they needed, therefore, was people, preferably people with dollars.

The church's situation appeared conducive to growth. Located in a suburban neighborhood that was seeing an influx of families, the church was easy to find and offered convenient and plentiful parking. The pastor was a good preacher and teacher, able to communicate biblical and theological concepts in a way that was insightful, inspiring, appropriately provocative, and relevant to the lives of members. *How could this church not grow?* That was seemingly the underlying message of the refrain "We want to grow." Yet the congregation was stuck.

At the two-thirds point of the retreat, one church leader raised a question I had heard before in strategic planning retreats. Surmising that I was the kind of new member the congregation would welcome, she asked, "If you lived in the area, would you join our church?"

When I said I would not be inclined to join the congregation, she looked shocked and asked why. Here's what I said:

"I have learned a lot about your congregation—reviewing the materials your pastor sent me before the retreat, and now being here for a day. You have much to offer, and you are very nice people.

"But I keep hearing," I added, "that you want me to join because you want to increase your membership numbers. You hope new members will contribute money to increase your budget. You hope new members will teach Sunday school and lead youth groups. In other words, the message I hear is that you want me to join for what I will do for you."

Then I said, "Now, if your message were more focused on how you want to grow in faith and mission, through worship and education, I could get excited about joining your church. And if I joined, then I would contribute money and might consider teaching Sunday school."

Many congregations feel a sense of urgency to grow. Unfortunately, they may not be aware of the messages they send about their motives. Too often, I fear, the desire to grow centers on a wish to sustain buildings, programming, and staff—and thus allow the congregation to remain as it has been. Less often, the desire to grow emanates from a vision of serving as a faith community for potential members, or of sharing the good news of a living, sovereign, and graceful God who creates, redeems, and sustains.

A Desire for Growth without Change

The only person who likes change is a wet baby. This statement, attributed to Mark Twain and written on an eight-and-a-half-by-eleven-inch sheet of paper, caught my attention as I browsed a bulletin board at Bethel Seminary in St. Paul, Minnesota. This saying has stayed with me as I have worked with pastors, Christian educators, youth ministers, music directors, church business administrators, lay leaders, and congregations.

The only person who likes change is a wet baby. A wet baby, it seems, has a sense of urgency that makes change attractive, if not imperative. A wet baby, particularly in the hands of a loving, caring, and trustworthy change agent, is willing to undergo the short-term vulnerability of change because the future, in a dry diaper, will be better than the present. Clearly, the trustworthiness of the change agent is crucial. This agent must be attentive to the baby's needs, must provide a safe environment that holds the baby's needs in trust, and must have the capacity to bring about change without dropping the baby. The church, it seems, can learn a great deal from wet babies—and from those who serve as change agents.

Many congregations find themselves in the throes of significant change. The culture is shifting, as are the demographics of communities and denominations. Congregations feel a sense of urgency to grow. What they do not feel is an urgency to *change* for the sake of that growth. And this absence of urgency creates a crisis.

Ronald Heifetz, a preeminent thinker in leadership theory and practice, asserts:

> In a crisis we tend to look for the wrong kind of leadership. We call for someone with answers, decision, strength, and a map of the future, someone who knows where we ought to be going—in short, someone who can make hard problems simple.[1]

To Heifetz, many of the problems we face are not so simple. Consequently, a primary task of leaders is assisting others to learn new ways, to develop their adaptive capacities so that they can respond to challenges appropriately and effectively. In a crisis, however, many people's capacities to change from old ways and to participate confidently in new initiatives diminish as their anxieties grow. Further, in crisis and change, the church both yearns for and resists effective leadership, particularly transformational leadership.

Many congregations want growth without change. Such growth is not likely, however. Where there is growth, there is typically change. And as most people recognize, where there is change, there is often conflict. Hoping to avoid conflict, many congregations remain ambivalent about whether they want to grow, for they know that change and possible conflict await them if they truly aspire to grow.

I have worked with several congregations in which tensions grew out of the desire for growth without change. Whether in urban areas, small towns, or rural settings, they observed the numerical growth of nearby congregations they characterized as "evangelical"—congregations that offered "contemporary" forms of worship. Leaders of stagnating or declining congregations have often wondered whether they ought to experiment with or adopt contemporary worship styles to appeal to those who otherwise would not be attracted to their church. In more than one situation, the scenario described below has unfolded.

First Church, a well-established congregation in a small community, has a history of influence and prestige in the community. Congregational membership, after peaking in the 1950s, has slowly declined over the past fifty years. Many explanations have been offered for the membership loss—the dislocation of churches in general from their prominent place in North American culture; competing opportunities and activities that draw people away from church involvement and membership; the seeming irrelevance to people's needs of much preaching, teaching, and ministry; and the lack of leadership in congregations.

Whatever the reasons, the elders of First Church decided that if it was to survive, it must become more "contemporary," particularly in its style of worship. Members felt great ambivalence about what they were getting themselves into. Congregational leaders reassured them that, with a pastor who could design and lead a new contemporary worship service, the congregation would appeal to younger individuals and families in the community, worship attendance would grow, and First

Church would regain the place of influence and prestige it had formerly enjoyed. Moreover, a contemporary worship service would be a doorway though which younger people and families would come into the church and get involved in the congregation's ministries, leading the faith community to a vitality not experienced for decades.

A strategic plan, centering on the worship life of the congregation, was developed. Lay leaders affirmed the pastor's gifts for contemporary worship and challenged him to use them wisely for the growth of the congregation. New vocal leaders and rock instrumentalists were recruited to replace the organist and choir. The new service was advertised and launched.

The contemporary service quickly attracted participants. Immediately, young families and teenagers already active in the congregation gravitated to the new service, finding it more meaningful than the traditional worship. Soon newcomers from the community began to visit the contemporary service, and a number of them decided to affiliate with First Church, at least for a while.

Within a year, the number of worshipers at the contemporary service matched the number at the traditional service. A small group of longtime members who were loyal to the church's rich traditions began to question whether the governing board had been wise to adopt the contemporary worship. Some voiced their concerns to the lay leaders:

"This new service is competing with our traditional worship service."

"We do not feel like one congregation anymore."

"Our image in the community is changing—we are becoming known as the church with a rock band."

"This is no longer my church."

As the contemporary service continued to thrive, the discomfort of a growing number of longtime members intensified. Some thought that adopting the new strategic plan was the worst decision the elders had ever made. Some believed that if the members, elders, and pastor would only try harder, the congregation could grow without a contemporary worship service and retain its identity as a traditional church. Some suspected that the pastor cared more about the newer and younger members than about the loyal stalwarts with decades of service. As time passed, these longtime members became more and more frustrated with the direction in which the congregation was moving.

Growth. Change. Conflict. These interrelated phenomena were present in equal measure, creating high levels of stress and anxiety within the congregation. It was only a matter of time before the tensions erupted and members found themselves divided over the preferred style of worship, the wisdom of the elders' decisions, the worship leadership of the pastor and musicians, and the effectiveness of the pastor's leadership in general.

The Difficulty of Unwanted Change

From First Church, we can see the difficulties that emerge in the wake of unwanted change. First, the defining points of the congregation were shifting as a result of the changes that came with the contemporary worship service. In significant ways, many longtime members were experiencing a loss of identity. Important dimensions of the congregation were becoming unfamiliar, even strange.

Second, church leaders hoped that their strategic plan, designed to achieve numerical growth, would motivate the congregation to support the changes inherent in a new style and service of worship. Strategic plans typically offer those who follow them a measure of predictability and control, perhaps enabling them to navigate their way into the future. First Church's plan, however, could not motivate longtime members to embrace change or provide them with the security of predictability. As anxiety in the congregation rose, interest in the strategic plan diminished. Moreover, many longtime members feared that the congregation would become unstable and chaotic, eventually spiraling out of control.

Third, the pace of change exceeded the capacity of many longtime members to embrace or at least to accept it. Leaders must be keenly aware that managing change is complicated by members' diverse expectations of an appropriate rate of change. If the pace of change that accompanied the growth of First Church's contemporary worship service was characterized as "ten miles per hour," some members would experience it as too fast, while other members, excited by opportunities for continued growth, would think it too slow. Differing perceptions of the pace of change can put leaders in a bind, as some regard their leadership as effective while others see it as ineffective.

Fourth, the relation of implemented change to the congregation's past is a significant factor in members' capacity to embrace change. To the degree that members perceive continuity between where the congregation has been and where it seems to be going, they may adapt to change. In contrast, change that seems discontinuous with the past may cause longtime members to resist. Leaders assisting congregations through change must be prepared to equip members to face the disequilibrium of change by attending to the pace and by reinforcing continuity between the future and the past.

Fifth, change increases a congregation's awareness of its existing vulnerabilities. Like caregivers with a "wet baby," leaders must be trustworthy change agents, sensitive to the diverse needs of the congregation as a whole and of its members. Like "wet babies," members must have a sense of urgency for change.

Sixth, leaders must assist members in acknowledging diverse reasons for urgency. At First Church, some members wanted to grow so that the congregation could recapture its former influence and prestige. Others wanted to grow to sustain the church's institutional structures. Others wanted to grow so they could serve the new families in the community surrounding the church. Others wanted to grow by adopting a new style of worship so that they could worship God in a way that reflected their own preferences. Naming and appreciating diverse sources of urgency may counter the vulnerability evoked by change in a congregation's life. The identification of the common concern of urgency to grow, with varying motives, may reinforce the congregation's cohesion, its willingness to trust leaders, and the confidence of a diversity of members in a moment of significant change.

Finally, leaders must remember that in a time of change congregations both yearn for and resist effective leadership. After all, leaders intend to evoke and lead effective change, not to thwart it. In the stress of change, especially deep and transformational change, congregations often look for ways to avoid the ambiguity and pain of change. Leaders who can provide "easy" answers generally are prized. But leaders who sincerely try to help congregations adapt to change may be regarded as ineffective. Those who serve as pastoral leaders may find themselves in a bind as they attempt to find a way to encourage needed change while maintaining their position as pastor of the congregation. There is seemingly only one escape from this bind—the pastor's decision to leave this congregation and move to another, where he or she is likely to experience a similar set of dynamics in due time.

Assisting a Congregation with Change

One of the first tasks in assisting a congregation with change is to explore its history of change. In many congregations, previous change efforts sparked negative consequences. Perhaps the intended change appeared to benefit primarily the pastor, staff, lay leaders, or small groups within the congregation. Maybe the pace of change was dramatically fast, overwhelming members and leaders who felt unable to measure up to the challenge. Perhaps the pace was dreadfully slow, creating a sense of atrophy in the congregation and diminishing members' motivation and passion for growth in ministry. Whatever the reasons, most congregations have had unpleasant experiences with change in the faith community. As a result, church members tend to have a built-in resistance to change, if not a deep-seated suspicion of it.

Even when change has been effective, someone always experiences a degree of loss—perhaps a loss of what is "normal," a loss of power and status, or a loss of place. Congregational leaders must remember that even when change generates positive results, it is always accompanied by pain for someone.

John Kotter, author of books and articles about change, offers helpful insights for those who assist congregations with change. In *Leading Change*, he identifies a correlation between *complacency* and *urgency* and challenges leaders to identify sources of each as a foundation for effecting change.[2] From his perspective, leaders often allow complacency within an organization to diminish the sense of urgency necessary to motivate people to change. One of the most important steps leaders must take to be effective, therefore, is to establish a sense of urgency.

I have a hunch that congregations generally look for leaders who will allow them to remain complacent in the face of declining membership numbers, diminishing participation in congregational life, and loss of cultural influence. If only we can select the right pastor and staff, if only we can elect wise governing board members, if only we can increase the commitment of our members—then we can delay any conversations about change, and we can maintain our identity. As the urgency to grow increases, the pressure to select leaders who can inspire growth without change intensifies. When these leaders are unable to meet the unrealistic expectations of those who might follow their lead, frustration builds.

To break the pattern of complacency that resists change, Kotter recommends two steps: (a) leaders must remove sources of complacency or minimize their impact, and (b) leaders must raise the level of urgency.[3] How leaders take these steps is one of their most crucial strategic decisions. Leaders are wise to understand that people's feelings determine how they view, experience, and respond to change.

In *The Heart of Change*, Kotter and Dan Cohen observe that the central issue in change is never strategy, structure, culture, or systems. Behavioral change happens when leaders speak to people's feelings. They point out: "People change what they do less because they are given *analysis* that shifts their *thinking* than because they are *shown* a truth that influences their *feelings*."[4]

Leaders who desire to stimulate change must be attentive to four sets of behaviors based in people's emotions—behaviors that prohibit change:

- Complacency, driven by false pride or arrogance.
- Immobilization, self-protection, a sort of hiding in the closet, driven by fear or panic.
- A you-can't-make-me-move deviance, driven by anger.
- Constant hesitation, driven by a pessimistic attitude.[5]

To be effective, pastoral leaders must identify the affective responses of others to unwanted change, and must work with them through those feelings that resist change. Until leaders do this, their efforts to bring about change will be blocked. Frustration will stymie growth in the congregation, and the pastor's leadership will be ineffective.

Closing Thoughts

Change is difficult, especially when it is transformational. Amid such change, congregational members and leaders may experience significant disruptions or losses as they navigate their way into the future.

In *The Challenge of Change in Organizations*, Nancy Barger and Linda Kirby identify a number of predictable losses people may experience during organizational change. They may lose:

+ familiar territory and people,
+ ownership,
+ structure and clarity,
+ an anticipated future,
+ meaning and direction,
+ control and predictability,
+ power or influence,
+ friends and colleagues,
+ networks and resources,
+ knowledge and expertise in a new situation, and
+ security and confidence.[6]

To bear the pain of such losses, congregational members and leaders must be helped to see the need for change. Naturally, the greater the anticipated change, the greater must be the identifiable benefit. Those who will encounter considerable pain as a result of change must see its purpose. Otherwise, they will perceive that it is "change for the sake of change."

This chapter has emphasized change in relation to *where we have been*. This emphasis is necessary, as many members and leaders are keenly aware of what they are leaving behind. The past is more vivid and defined for them than the future is. And they generally are more invested in and attached to where they have been than where they are going.

Change is difficult. It challenges the adaptability, flexibility, and resilience of congregations in a rapidly changing world. On the verge of change, leaders cannot command members to *go from*. They can invite members to *come to* and, at their best, they can assist members in finding the inspiration needed to manage the pain of change. Ideally, inspiration comes as members and leaders discern how God is calling and leading the congregation forward, and as they respond to "the call to change" as a call to faithful following.

Later chapters emphasize change in relation to *where we are going*. First, however, I will examine more closely the need for change in relation to the losses many congregations have experienced in recent years. Drawing upon perspectives of attachment theory, chapter 2 explores the nature of loss experienced in congregations depending on the degree to which people and groups have been attached to what they have lost or anticipate losing.

For Reflection and Discussion

1. What are the key defining points for your congregation? How do these defining points differ for various members and groups of members?

2. What are the most significant opportunities and challenges facing the congregation? If the congregation responds to these, what changes will it encounter?

3. What *sources of complacency* are likely to frustrate and inhibit effective change? What *sources of urgency* are likely to motivate and facilitate change?

4. What stressors and anxieties are likely to emerge if the congregation changes? What feelings do you anticipate that members will have in the midst of change? What feelings do you anticipate you will have as a leader?

5. As they meet change, what do congregational members need from and expect of you? What do you need from and expect of each other as leaders in the congregation?

6. How are you discerning the calling and leading of God to move in a new direction?

CHAPTER TWO

The Depths of Loss in the Midst of Change

People do not resist change, per se. People resist loss.
RONALD A. HEIFETZ AND MARTY LINSKY[1]

The profound statement above captures the essence of how people may experience change. It reframes the resistance that congregational leaders meet when they try to prompt substantial change in the life of a faith community. It reminds leaders of the emotional processes that drive members' responses to change. And it crisply restates the understanding that where there is change, there is loss—at least for some individuals.

When congregational leaders encounter members' resistance to change, they may be tempted to attribute it to a variety of sources: idolatrous loyalty to the traditions of the past; a desire to hold onto power that comes from positions in the congregation; a lack of confidence in the future, or in the leaders who point toward the future and the change needed if the church is to thrive; a lack of openness to the movement of the Spirit of God; stubbornness, rigidity, and defensiveness—the list is endless. In response, leaders may consider a number of options for countering resistance. They may confront the resisters, perhaps using their own power and authority to reinforce their position. They may seek compromise where incremental change is possible, hoping that a smaller change will not alienate members from the church or the church's leaders. They may accommodate the preferences of the resisting members, deciding that change is not worth the fight it will provoke. They may choose to avoid the situation altogether, hoping it will go away if they ignore it.[2]

Heifetz and Linsky sensitize us to more complex reasons for resistance—resistance born of loss rather than change per se. This insight leads us to respond differently to people resisting change. Rather than focusing on positions and sources of resistance, we see others as individuals suffering loss. As we empathize with them in their loss, we quickly see that each resisting person is a *grieving* person.

With sensitivity to the interrelationships of change, resistance, loss, and grief, this chapter explores three phenomena:

1. The church is experiencing many losses.
2. In the face of loss, the church is grieving profoundly—and the nature and depth of the grief are shaped significantly by the church's attachment to the things it has lost, is losing, or fears losing.
3. In a time of loss and grief congregations expect, and feel more keenly, the need for effective leadership—leadership that will minimize the loss, reverse the trends of loss, and perhaps yield growth without change, or change without pain.

Chapter 3 explores a fourth and related phenomenon: a key challenge for leadership is easing a congregation's movement through loss and grief and helping it deepen its capacity to *attach anew.*

A Backdrop of Loss

Many congregations find themselves in crisis. Their crises may be related to significant changes in the surrounding community or culture, or within their own walls and structures. The heart of their crisis centers on years of accumulated losses that have resulted in unbearable pain, fluctuating levels of self-confidence, and insecurity about the future. As you consider the losses other congregations have suffered, think about your own congregation's losses.

Loss of Members

Many congregations remember a time when they had more members, younger members, and more involved members. Over time, these congregations have become aware that their members are fewer, older, and less active in the church. Looking ahead, members and leaders fear that the average age of members will continue to rise; fewer members will remain, and those members will be less active as aging stalwarts are not replaced by younger volunteers. Linked to this loss is the fear that a time will come when the congregation can no longer keep its doors open.

Congregations must often deal with the loss of valued members remembered for their service as pillars of the church. When the congregation was vital and growing, these people provided significant leadership that was never replaced after the "glory days" had passed.

Loss of Congregation's Centrality for Members

In the past, congregations could count on members to make church involvement a priority. Gone are the days when the church was the religious and social center of the community. Members have many more choices to fill their Sunday mornings and evenings, whether on the soccer field or in the coffee shop; and congregations increasingly compete for the affections, commitments, and loyalties of their members. While members of all ages have more choices, it is the loss of youth that is most lamented, as if the choices made by youth and their parents were the primary factor in the congregation's decline. No longer do congregations occupy a privileged place in the lives of most members. Church appears instead as another item in the social cafeteria from which people may pick and choose what matches their appetites.

The loss of members' commitment has an impact on other aspects of the life and ministry of congregations. As members seemingly feel less obligation to the church and a life of faith, their stewardship of time and financial giving changes. Moreover, newer generations of members are less literate biblically and in the basic tenets of faith, as well as less familiar with the history of the congregation and its treasured traditions. As a result, some congregational leaders increasingly wonder about the centrality of Christ in the lives of members and their families—and yet, they do not know how to raise questions of faith and commitment, fearing they will be perceived as judgmental and increasingly alienate members from the congregation.

Loss of Pastors and Staff Members

Many congregations have fond memories of former pastors and staff members who provided significant leadership at a time when congregational vitality was evident in membership and attendance statistics, the range of programming for all ages, the number of missionaries supported, and the proportion of the budget given to benevolent causes. Some of these pastors and staff members served long tenures.

At First United Presbyterian Church of Alliance, Ohio, where I served as associate pastor from 1986 to 1990, John V. Stephens had served as pastor from 1929 until his retirement in 1963. He had led the congregation during the crash of the stock market in 1929 and the Great Depression that followed, through World War II, the Cold War, the Korean War, and early phases of the Vietnam conflict. In the 1950s the congregation grew under his leadership to nearly sixteen hundred members. When I began my pastoral service in 1986, membership totaled 941, and longtime members continued to remember Dr. Stephens with great fondness, associating his retirement and the loss of his pastoral leadership with the slow decline of membership numbers.

Other congregations have rich memories of those who have served them faithfully and effectively as Christian educators, music directors, youth ministers, and administrative staff members. No longer with the congregation, these leaders are missed because of the quality of their service and leadership and the degree of congregational vitality associated with their tenure.

An increasing number of congregations can no longer afford a paid staff of the size they maintained when financial resources were more abundant. Larger congregations have reduced staff size and are poignantly aware that they cannot support the staff-led ministry they enjoyed in the past—and they regard such changes as significant losses. Smaller congregations have come to realize that (a) if they retain a full-time pastor, they will be unable to provide financial support for programming and mission; (b) if they reduce pastoral service from a full-time to a part-time position, they will have a reduced pastoral presence and ministry and will attract fewer candidates who desire to serve as their pastor; and (c) if they can no longer afford a seminary-trained pastor, they must look at alternative models for pastoral leadership. In each of these scenarios, the loss of people and positions is accompanied by the loss of a past—a time when the congregation seemed healthier and more vital.

Loss of Traditions

The loss of a congregation's traditions is perhaps most obvious in the structure and content of worship. After all, many congregations view as their most significant defining mark the gathering of the faith community in worship. While recognizing that worship focuses on praising God and proclaiming the Word, congregations believe they can measure their vitality by the numbers of people participating in worship each week and the dollars received in the weekly offering. The way a congregation worships may also determine how it is perceived by other congregations and the community.

Other defining marks may be seen in a congregation's historic emphases in education, mission, witness, outreach, and social justice. With a loss of members and leaders, many congregations believe they have a decreased capacity for ministry and that they lack the visionary leadership to continue such emphases. Moreover, as some congregations have attempted to appeal to younger generations, they have de-emphasized some of these defining marks of the past as they have aspired to "reinvent" themselves. This de-emphasis has underscored the dynamics of change in congregational life and has deepened the sense of loss felt by some members.

Loss of Structural Supports

When congregational membership was growing, structural supports were critical in the development and operation of programs. Church boards, committees, task forces, and ministry teams provided valuable service and leadership that ensured the vitality of congregations. These service opportunities also deepened the commitment of members to diverse ministries, cultivated a culture of shared leadership, and provided rich opportunities for membership formation, Christian education, congregational fellowship, service to the community, and mission outreach.

For some members, the proliferation of programming has diminished the central place of worship in the life of the congregation, as the "success" of a congregation has come to be assessed more by the number of program participants than by the quality of worship. To other members, increased programming has had at least one disturbing effect: leading many members to value what they can *get* from the church more than what they can *give* to it.

Many congregations have faced significant challenges in trying to sustain the structural supports that made possible the development of their ministries. Fewer people volunteer to serve in the congregation, perhaps because the church has become less central to their lives. Some longtime volunteers have exhausted themselves and refuse to take on new leadership roles.

The loss of volunteers makes it harder for congregations to recruit and retain members and leaders of educational classes, youth groups, children's ministries, and committees and ministry teams. In too many cases, pastors, staff members, and other congregational leaders fear that they are filling chairs with bodies rather than identifying, using, and deepening members' gifts and passions in the church's diverse ministries.

In connectional denominations, many congregations historically have appreciated the structural supports of regional and national governing bodies that provide significant resources for worship, Christian education, children's and youth ministries, young-adult ministries, stewardship, mission and outreach, and evangelism. Within these denominations, congregations have felt connected to a larger church, and through the larger church to the world. Denominational ties have also connected congregational leaders to one another, whether as pastors, staff members, elders, or deacons. As financial and human resources for regional and national governing bodies have declined, however, the capacity of these agencies to provide resources for congregations has diminished as well. Accordingly, congregations in connectional denominations increasingly find themselves on their own, without structural supports that earlier played an important role.

Loss of Status in the Community

Many congregations historically enjoyed power and influence in their communities, whether in rural areas, small towns, or large cities. Church leaders often served as leaders in civic organizations, held visible and powerful roles in the community, and were identified as pillars of the community.

In many cases, the status of the congregation and its leaders in the community has been diminished, if not lost.

Beyond the local community, many congregational members and leaders believe that the church once held more influence within North American culture—spiritually, morally, socially, politically, and economically. Many perceive that the church has lost its influence and clout, its prominence, and its relevance—whether as a result of the decline of Christendom, the cultural disestablishment of the church, the erosion of the church's prestige when congregational scandals became public, or the church's complacency at a time when congregations were growing.

Loss of Stability

All of the previously identified losses have resulted in a loss of stability for many congregations. These congregations seem less durable than in the past. No longer do they function as communities for restoration and renewal. Instead, their members and leaders typically feel vulnerable, insecure, and uncertain about the future.

For some members and leaders, the loss of stability has intensified as they have experienced change, especially unwanted change. Too often, the loss of stability has resulted in a fragile congregational unity that is increasingly susceptible to "church fights." Naturally, such battles increase levels of instability and vulnerability, yielding more anxiety and a thinning veneer of trust among members and leaders.

Loss of Confidence

Enduring multiple losses and changes, many congregations have found their confidence eroding in significant dimensions of the faith community: leaders' effectiveness, members' commitment, denominational cohesion, and the faith community's relevance to the culture. Such a loss of confidence is seen when:

a. Members lament that the congregation is not attracting the best and brightest leaders;

b. leaders mourn that members are not as committed to their faith as members were in a previous era, because of the choices they are making about participation in congregational life;

c. members and leaders grieve the divisions that agitate many denominations as partisan groups quarrel over theological and social issues; and

d. congregations lament the increasing gap between their identity and ministries and the communities and culture in which they live.

In lament, members may question whether leaders have the capacity to lead the congregation into a better future. Pastors and staff members may increasingly feel like mere employees of the church, defined more by their position descriptions than by their calling. In turn, lay leaders may decide that they are no longer going to waste their time and energy in a congregation preoccupied with lament.

As congregations are overwhelmed by loss and change, the ebbing of confidence creates significant breaches in the relationships at the heart of their identity. Questions of trust, respect, and credibility diminish congregations' capacity for ministry. Over time, loss of confidence has immobilized congregational leaders and members, preventing them from identifying and pursuing creative and hopeful solutions to their troubles.

Loss of Energy for Ministry

Congregations that have experienced many losses often have less energy, vitality, and passion for ministry. They are tired and depressed.

Lacking a sense of purpose and a vision, these congregations seem more confident of their continuing decline than of the possibility of their renewal or rebirth. Visitors and observers are likely to perceive the congregation as a community that is "holding on," more desperate for new blood than for new life, and as a people of passionless faith whose routines reflect monotonous ritual rather than the celebration of abundant life.

Too many congregations have come to believe that their best days are behind them. Accordingly, they cling to what they can of the past and the present and exhibit less capacity to be creative, flexible, and adaptable in responding to opportunities and challenges. And since a "clinging" stance diminishes a congregation's capacity to discern a different future, even congregations that undertake a "discernment process" may discover a preference for reclaiming the lost identity and ministry of the past.

Loss of Identity

Many a congregation that has endured a string of losses hears members lamenting, "We're not the church we used to be." The congregation has lost members and leaders. It has lost the central place it once held in the lives of its members and the community. It has lost traditions and the support structures crafted to reinforce such traditions. It has lost power and influence. And in the destabilization of congregational systems, members have lost confidence in themselves and others, energy and purpose as a people of faith, passion for the ministries to which they feel called and for which they feel responsible, and hope for a better future.

"Who are we now?" such congregations ask. The ethos in which many congregations once thrived, regardless of their size, has changed. An era has ended. On some level, many congregations are keenly aware that how they discern and live into the future, not how they engaged in ministry in past years, will determine their viability and vitality.

Since even necessary change is difficult, many congregations mourn, grieving the loss of the past as they struggle with questions of who they are to become.

A Pause to Reflect

1. What losses has your congregation sustained?
2. Which losses are having the most significant impact on your congregation?
3. What effect are these losses having on your congregation? On its members? On its leaders?
4. Complete this statement: "If _____ were no longer a part of my congregation, I would feel a significant loss."

Unlocking the Depths of Loss: The "Key" of Attachment

Congregations that profoundly grieve their losses are looking for leadership—typically, leadership to fix things. Actually, however, what they need are leaders who understand them and their deep sense of loss.

As leaders consider the losses and grief embedded in the congregations they serve, it is crucial that they consider the *degrees of attachment* to those dimensions of congregational life that have been lost or that people fear losing. John Bowlby, a pioneer in the field of attachment theory, and other attachment theorists offer constructive perspectives on the relationships between attachment, loss, and grief.

Simply put, the more attached we are to those people, places, or things that are meaningful to us and that perhaps "define" us, the more their loss, or anticipated loss, will evoke grief for us. Individuals have differing degrees of attachment to various people, places, and things:

- Relationally, we are attached to mothers and fathers, sisters and brothers, spouses, sons and daughters, extended family members, mentors and teachers, and friends.
- Materially, we are attached to homes, cars, wardrobes, special collections, and other possessions.

+ Vocationally, we are attached to jobs, careers, and callings that use our gifts and interests in meaningful and life-giving ways.
+ Sentimentally, we are attached to autographed baseball cards from childhood, a first pair of ballet shoes, the pen-and-pencil set received as a graduation gift, the dried roses from a first anniversary—items whose treasure is defined largely by the memories and relationships to which they point.

Likewise, members of congregations experience meaningful attachments. People may be attached to:

+ Pastors, Christian educators, choir directors, youth leaders, and other people who have served as models of faith and discipleship and have expressed interest in members' well-being at critical times.
+ Sanctuaries, especially those distinguished by beautiful stained-glass windows and historic pipe organs.
+ Worship traditions, educational programs, mission and outreach, evangelism, and social-justice emphases.
+ Pulpit Bibles given in memory of parents, wooden crosses that sit on communion tables, Christmas ornaments made by generations of children, portraits of former pastors and staff members, paintings by young-adult members who fought but eventually succumbed to terminal diseases.

Congregational leaders must deepen their awareness of the differing degrees of attachment individuals have to other people, places, and things and the nature of losses in congregational life. With any given loss and the change it signifies, some members of a congregation will experience deep grief, others moderate grief, and still others little if any grief. Each of these subgroups needs a different response from leaders. Each has a different expectation of what constitutes effective leadership.

Recognizing that not all losses count the same, leaders are wise to understand that *attachment* is the key to understanding the complex dynamics of loss and grief in congregations and to discerning why some members grieve certain changes and losses while others do not. From Bowlby's theoretical base, the following principles will help congregational leaders understand the relationships among attachment, change and loss, and grief.

1. *Attaching to other people, places, or things is an instinctive behavior.* From his research with young children, coupled with other theorists' research into attachment behaviors among primates, Bowlby observed that attaching to others is foundational to human behavior. It is our natural instinct to attach. We are "wired" to attach.

Painful experiences involving those people with whom we have primary relationships, whether in childhood or later in life, may recondition this instinct and damage our capacity to attach in healthy ways. To avoid future pain, we may adopt behaviors that attempt to moderate our attachment needs to protect ourselves. Still, our instinct is to attach.

2. *Attaching behavior is lifelong behavior.* Although Bowlby's theory was based largely upon the relationships of young children to their mothers, he extrapolated his theory into adolescence and adulthood and emphasized the developmental dimensions of attachment behavior.

To Bowlby, the quality of attachments to one or more parents remains significant during adolescence and adulthood. He also observed that when we become members of an older generation, attachment behaviors typically are redirected toward people of younger generations.[3]

3. *Significant attachments may offer a secure base—for children, youth, adults, and congregations.* From the perspective of attachment theory, an individual or group that serves as a "secure base" provides a point of reference—a defining point—from which we can reach out and explore new possibilities, knowing that when our fears and anxieties begin to overwhelm us, we may return to the secure base for comfort, safety, and reassurance. For a young child, one or both parents

may provide such a base. Over time, a child in healthy circumstances will internalize this base, although he or she will continue to need external reference points to reinforce the inner base of security throughout life.

For congregations, a secure base may be represented by its past, particularly periods of congregational stability, growth, and vitality. During such times, it seemed easier for congregations to reach out, to explore new possibilities, and to take risks. In such an era the rich traditions of congregations and the leadership of pastors, staff members, and lay leaders provided a reference point to which a congregation could return for comfort, safety, and reassurance.

The concept of a secure base is foundational for understanding church members and congregations. When a secure base continues to be responsible and responsive, people's attachment to it is deepened. The reliability of a secure base also allows people and congregations to explore the present and future boldly and confidently.

In contrast, a secure base that becomes unpredictable or unresponsive breeds ambivalence in people and congregations. They wonder whether it is safe to reach out, to explore new possibilities, and to take risks. If the security of the base is diminished or threatened, congregations and members suffer anxiety. If a secure base is lost, they grieve. Whether the base becomes insecure or disappears, they feel anger.[4]

4. *The disruption of a significant attachment to people, places, or things generates feelings of separation anxiety in individuals and congregations.* Bowlby identifies a predictable sequence of behavior commonly referred to as "separation anxiety" that occurs when bonds of attachment are disrupted.[5]

In the first phase, *protest*, a person expresses anger in an attempt to restore affectional bonds that are disrupted. Young children who realize that their mother or father is about to go, leaving them—perhaps with a babysitter, or in a hospital or day care center or even the church nursery—yell and scream instinctively, hoping that their cries will cause the parent to return. Members of congregations who face the loss of important attachments also may protest, whether quietly or loudly, hoping that valued relationships and order will be restored.

In the second phase, *despair*, people vacillate between feelings of hope and hopelessness. As their ambivalence grows, their levels of anxiety and panic rise. After all, the expressions of protest have not restored the ruptured bond with the object of attachment. These dynamics are applicable to congregations experiencing broken attachments and painful losses.

In the third phase, *detachment*, a person or congregation no longer protests or expresses feelings of despair. Children lose interest in those people who have not responded to their cries, becoming emotionally apathetic and disengaged.

Members of congregations also may lose interest and become apathetic. In response, congregational leaders may wrongly perceive that the "storm has passed" and that members have adjusted to their losses. Members who have detached have not, however, "moved on" as such. Instead they have relinquished the bond of attachment—not in a healthy way but in a defensive posture, seeking self-protection to avoid being vulnerable or hurt again. These people have suppressed their anger and anxiety, and have disengaged themselves emotionally from others and from the congregation as a system.

Responding to members' diverse expressions of separation anxiety is a complex challenge for leaders. First, individual members have different attachments, or bases of security and identity. As a result, congregations and their subgroups typically are experiencing various losses concurrently. Second, while some members are protesting a specific loss, other members are responding with despair to the same loss, and still others have become detached, or emotionally disengaged, in relation not only to the particular loss but often to other dimensions of congregational life as well.

Congregational leaders will be challenged to respond to these losses, the disruption of attachments, the compromise of secure bases, and varied expressions of separation anxiety.

The intensity of expressed feelings will be shaped by the degree of attachment to the secure bases that have been lost or that people anticipate losing.

5. *Through experiences with objects of attachment, individuals and congregations have developed identifiable attachment patterns that have shaped their personalities, conditioned their perspectives on relationships, and affected their behavior toward others.*[6] What we have experienced as children, as adolescents, and as adults "comes with us to church" and affects our capacity for healthy attachments in congregational life.

A pattern of *secure* attachment develops when people have positive experiences with their objects of attachment, including the healthy restoration of bonds that are threatened or disrupted. Secure bases remain secure. Over time, people internalize bases of security, although they need and appreciate external reference points that continue to reinforce this inner strength. Accordingly, they tend to have high levels of ego strength and resiliency and generally are happier and less demanding than more anxious people.

A pattern of *anxious resistant* attachment emerges when people have ambivalent experiences with their objects of attachment.[7] Perhaps a parent or both parents were unavailable or unresponsive at significant points in their early childhood. Perhaps affectional bonds to parents were fractured during adolescence, when the defining points offered by parents and within families of origin came into conflict with developing peer relationships. Perhaps painful experiences in dating, marriage, or divorce have diminished the security of the internalized base. Whatever the reasons, this pattern creates a high level of anxiety within people who desire a deep affectional bond, at the same time fear it, and sometimes cling to other people, places, or things as a manifestation of their ambivalence.

A pattern of *anxious avoidant* attachment is evident when people have had alienating experiences with their objects of attachment. They have been "burned" by those in whom they have placed their trust. As a result, they have no confidence that others will be available, reliable, and responsive to their needs. Expecting rejection, they have learned to become self-sufficient. Yet this defensive stance is also born of anxiety that is buried so deeply that the avoidant person generally has lost touch with it. Such a pattern generally leads people to disregard the value of relationships. Typically, avoidant people distance themselves from others. Periodically, they "bully" others in an effort to exert power and control.

6. *The attachments that congregational members and leaders seek or experience in faith communities are often related to experiences of attachment in their personal lives.* Professor of psychology Lee Kirkpatrick offers valuable insights into the relationship between one's personal experiences with attachment and their impact on religious faith and practices.[8] First, children who have not experienced healthy relationships, or *secure attachments*, with their parents may later seek these relationships elsewhere. Seeking "substitute attachment figures," they may turn to faith, hoping that God will fill the gap experienced in their relationships with their mothers and fathers. Or they may turn to a congregation in the hope that its members and leaders will provide the love, acceptance, support, and nurture not experienced in familial relationships. To them, God or the congregation has the potential to compensate for affectional bonds they lack and to provide the "safe haven" for which they have yearned.

Second, people who have developed secure, anxiously resistant, or anxiously avoidant patterns of attachment in their families of origin and in other significant relationships may seek to replicate these patterns in relationships within the faith community. People with histories and patterns of secure attachments and healthy relationships may anticipate and seek similar experiences in relation to God and within the congregation. People with histories of insecure attachments, whether resistant or avoidant, may also seek the types of experiences with which they are familiar in relating to God and to the congregation. Further, they have developed defense mechanisms that allow them to survive without the risk of reaching out and being rejected again.

7. *Patterns of attachment may change over time.* Attaching to other people, places, or things is an instinctive, lifelong behavior, and over time identifiable patterns of attachment emerge. These patterns of attachment may change. Sometimes changes are due largely to the influence of significant relationships or to one's environment. Sometimes positive changes in patterns of attachment arc sought intentionally.

Bowlby identifies ways in which therapeutic processes may benefit those whose negative experiences of attachment or separation have hindered healthy personality development.[9] Effective therapists may provide clients with a *secure base* in which they may explore themselves, past experiences, current circumstances, and future possibilities for healthier affectional bonds and relationships. Effective therapeutic processes may assist people in recognizing how they themselves have contributed to their unhealthy relationships. Therapists may use the therapeutic relationship itself to explore how their clients are replicating expressions of trust or mistrust from other relationships or countering past behaviors with new patterns of interaction. Therapeutic processes may help people understand how they get themselves into situations that reenact previous experiences, whether in an unconscious attempt to relive them or with the hope of redeeming them.

Effective congregational leaders do not attempt to engage in "therapy" with other leaders and members. Nevertheless, they do recognize that religious faith and congregational life may be redemptive for people who have experienced broken relationships and who struggle with questions of trust and safety. Congregations may provide people with a base of security in which they experience healing from past wounds and develop healthier patterns of attachment to others. Naturally, this takes time and does not come easily for people—or for congregations.

A Pause to Reflect

Using the table below, identify actual or anticipated losses that have occurred in your congregation. With each loss, identify people or groups that have had varying degrees of attachment to the loss. Identify the evidence of their attachment.

Losses— Actual or Anticipated	People or Groups with Significant Attachment— Evidence of Their Attachment	People or Groups with Moderate Attachment— Evidence of Their Attachment	People or Groups with Little/No Attachment— Evidence of Their Attachment

A Yearning for Effective Leaders

In the face of loss and grief, the need for and expectations of leadership increase. In some congregations, members expect great things from leaders. The pressures to perform and produce become more intense as the pain of loss increases. In many congregations with which I have consulted, members believe that if only they can work harder, they can avert the changes they face and the losses they fear. The tendency to keep busy, however, is often an attempt to avoid the reality of change, the depth of loss, and the pain of grief.

In these circumstances, many congregations seek leaders who will provide easy answers—preferably, a map to the past so that they may recover what has been lost. Effective leaders, however, do not lead backward but forward. In the hearts of those members most attached to the past, leaders seem to be trying to move them further from their secure base. When leaders are effective, the leadership for which many congregations yearn is not the leadership they will receive—and that they truly need.

Ronald Heifetz reminds us that effective leaders assist others in learning new ways to respond effectively to challenges. These critical actions are more than tasks to pursue and complete. They build upon relationships that are crucial in the dynamic interplay of leader and follower—relationships born of mutual faith and trust.

Given the multiple sources of change and loss, congregational leaders are called to roles and functions that members do not recognize as marks of effective leadership. Leaders are called to stand with members and to assist in seeing, naming, and sharing the pain of loss. They must genuinely empathize with members, understanding the complexity of attachments and losses that various people and subgroups of the congregation are experiencing. They must communicate care and understanding, and create or deepen a congregational ethos in which varied responses to change and loss may be understood and accepted. And they must enable a process through which congregations grieve their losses and deepen their capacity to *attach anew.*

Deepening Sensitivities for Effective Leadership

Congregations are looking for leadership during a time of significant change. To be effective, leaders must remember:

+ Many congregations are experiencing multiple losses. Yet the degree of pain associated with these losses varies among individuals.
+ In the face of these losses, congregations are grieving profoundly.
+ The depth of these losses, and the intensity of the resulting grief, is shaped by members' degrees of attachment to the things the congregation has lost, is losing, or fears losing.
+ In the throes of change, loss, and grief, many congregations yearn for effective leaders. Yet the most effective response of leaders is likely to differ from what people expect.

As congregational leaders become more sensitive to the dynamics of change, loss, attachment, and grief, they are wise to see that loss helps us recognize the depths of our "defining points," those things to which we are deeply attached. The experience of loss may sensitize us to what we often have not sufficiently honored, valued, or nurtured over time. With new perspectives on attachment, leaders and congregations may grow in their appreciation of what is important to them—and to others—and in their capacity to cherish their affectional bonds to people, places, and things.

As leaders grow in their sensitivity to attachment and loss, they are wise to recognize their own feelings about the changes and losses suffered by the congregations they serve.

Becoming more responsive to others' emotional processes is an important function of leadership. Equally important is leaders' awareness of their own emotional processes—to the ways in which they are working out their own broken attachments and unresolved losses.

Finally, as congregational leaders grow in their sensitivity to people struggling with breaking or broken attachments, they are wise to become more aware of how race, class, gender, culture, and other influences may shape the ways various people perceive and experience dynamics of change, loss, attachment, and grief. Such sensitivity is especially important as congregations become, or aspire to become, more diverse, seeking to welcome those whose backgrounds and identities are different from their own.

For Reflection and Discussion

1. How would you describe the state of your congregation as it experiences changes and losses?

2. Amid changes and losses, what expectations do congregational members seem to have of leaders? What expectations do congregational leaders seem to have of each other?

3. What "adaptive capacities" do congregational *members* need to develop to respond effectively to the challenges at hand?

4. What "adaptive capacities" do congregational *leaders* need to develop if they are to respond effectively to these challenges?

5. How and where do you perceive the activity of God as your congregation experiences changes and losses?

CHAPTER THREE

The Pain of Change

... so that you may not grieve as others do who have no hope.

1 Thessalonians 4:13b

Grieving. Hoping. These powerful emotions may coexist, seemingly competing for dominance in our hearts and minds and souls. In the juxtaposition of grief and hope, we may experience a degree of anxiety, particularly when our grieving becomes so intense that it disempowers our capacity to hope.

Looking back, my first experience of grieving, of *really* grieving, took place on August 12, 1990, the Sunday I concluded my ministry as an associate pastor at First United Presbyterian Church in Alliance, Ohio. I was scheduled to preach that day. Then, after a quick lunch, I would be departing for Louisville, Kentucky, to begin graduate studies in pastoral care and counseling. I was excited about what lay before me and what the future might bring. But first I was to preach and to say goodbye to the congregation I had served for four years.

My four years of ministry there were special, and I knew that the congregation and community would always hold a tender place in my heart. This was my first call, the place where

I was ordained to pastoral ministry in 1986. My two sons, Drew and Stefan, were born in Alliance and baptized at First Church. My relationships with the members were deep, and through shared experiences in worship, education, mission, and fellowship we had become close. Clearly, I would miss this congregation and its members. What I did not know was how much.

On my final Sunday in Alliance, I selected 1 Corinthians 13 as the text for my sermon on "What I Hope For." My message would include a statement of my faith and would express appreciation for the ways I had grown in my faith and capacity for ministry and in my relationships with the congregation's members—or better yet, my *friendships* with its members. I decided to preach from a rocking chair I had brought from home—the comfortable, creaky rocker in which I would often sit and hold my young children while telling or reading them a story. It was a "sacred" chair to me—perfect, I thought, for the message that would conclude my ministry in Alliance.

After reading the Scripture passage from the pulpit, I walked down to the rocking chair, directly in front of the communion table. I sat down and opened my mouth—and no words came out. *None.* The congregation was stunned, as was I. I could utter no words at all—I, an extroverted person who ordinarily spoke easily and rapidly.

And then the tears came—streaming down my cheeks with nothing to hold them back and no handkerchief to dry them. Three minutes passed in silence. As I wept, I saw some members of the congregation beginning to do the same. The pastor with whom I had worked so closely walked over to me, knelt, placed his hand on my arm, and indicated that it was OK; I did not need to proceed with the sermon. I responded that I was fine, that my tears reflected my love for the congregation and its members, and that I would be ready to preach soon.

Eventually, the tears ceased, at least for a few hours. I preached. The congregation applauded. We exchanged hugs and good wishes after the service. My family and I enjoyed a quick lunch with another family in the church. And then I climbed into the driver's seat of the rental truck, and we began a six-hour drive to Louisville—a drive that seemed much longer, and during which the tears began to flow again. Before this day, I had on occasion been sad or disappointed. But this was grief, raw and unexpected. And in its powerful grip, I lost my voice.

Within a year of my move from Alliance to Louisville, I was working on a master's thesis on attachment theory. I did not select this topic for research because of my relationship to the congregation in Alliance or because of my grief at the conclusion of this ministry. But the topic did help me understand why my grief was so powerful—namely, because of my deep attachment to the congregation and its members. They had provided me, for my first four years of ordained ministry, a secure base from which I could explore the possibilities and realities of ministry, knowing that I could rely on a faith community of comfort, safety, and reassurance. Over time, I had increasingly internalized the security of the base. These people were special, and I would miss them dearly.

No one likes to grieve. But amid loss, change that generates loss, and broken or breaking attachments, we feel the powerful grip of grief. And it hurts. At such times, leaders are challenged to help congregations grieve, so that they can begin to accept the reality of the loss and to develop the capacity to attach anew. Clearly, this is not the expression of leadership that most congregations expect, want, or will readily accept. Instead, they yearn for leadership that will minimize their losses and enable them to avoid the pain of grief.

Effective leaders, however, help congregations name losses, grieve well, and develop the capacity to attach anew. And they help congregations develop a vision for the future that will guide and inspire them. While these congregations will grieve, they will do so with hope.

Naming and Grieving Losses

Why is it important to name and grieve losses? Is it not easier simply to acknowledge our losses and to move on? Some congregational members and leaders express such sentiments in a time of loss, believing that attending to grief is a misdirection of energy, a misplacement of priorities, and a poor use of time.

Losses that are not appropriately named and grieved remain buried, however, as do the intense feelings associated with them. And although we may look as if we are "moving forward," we remain stuck in the emotional processes of loss, unable to reinvest ourselves in the life and ministry of the congregation.

Naturally, grieving takes energy. It takes time and effort. For those willing to invest themselves in grieving, the healing experienced thereby revitalizes their quality of life and their capacity to engage in meaningful relationships and purposeful ministry. Indeed, these people are most able to move forward.

A number of theorists have provided helpful frameworks that assist congregations and people in naming and grieving their losses. John Bowlby, whose theory of the relationship of attachment to loss shaped the previous chapter, describes four phases of mourning:

1. Numbing, which may be interrupted by outbursts of intense feelings.
2. Yearning and searching for the lost person or object.
3. Disorganization and despair.
4. Reorganization, to some degree.[1]

The amount of time required and the intensity of each of these phases vary from person to person. Additional variables that may shape mourning are

a. the nature of the relationship to the bereaved person,
b. the age and gender of the bereaved person,
c. the causes of and circumstances surrounding the loss,

    d.   the social and psychological circumstances affecting the bereaved person around the time of the loss, and

    e.   the personality of the bereaved person, including capacities for and patterns of attachment to others and the way he or she responds to stress.[2]

Many congregational members and leaders are more familiar with the overlapping perspectives of other authors who have written about the processes of naming and grieving losses. Psychiatrist Elisabeth Kubler-Ross, the most familiar theorist, identified five stages that terminal patients and their families typically experience to cope with impending death:

+ denial and isolation,
+ anger,
+ bargaining,
+ depression, and
+ acceptance.[3]

Kubler-Ross emphasized that these stages may last for differing periods of time and that although one stage may replace another, the stages may also coexist.[4] In considering these stages, particularly bargaining, it is important to remember that they are more relevant in anticipatory loss and grief than in loss itself.

Less familiar are the perspectives of pastoral psychologist Wayne Oates, who in *Your Particular Grief* provides valuable insights into grieving. Among his contributions to our capacities to name and understand grieving are the following ideas:

1.   Each person grieves differently from others. Yet each person's grief is not so different that he or she cannot find fellowship with others in suffering.[5]

2.   Grief is shaped by multiple variables:

    a.   the unique character of the relationship with another person, place, or thing—including the depth and length of the relationship;

b. the manner of loss;

c. previous experiences with grief;

d. the timeliness or untimeliness of the loss; and

e. the spiritual resources of the mourner.[6]

3. While "time may heal," it is important to know *how* people heal over time. Grieving occurs in stages:

a. shock,

b. numbness,

c. a mixture of belief and disbelief,

d. depression and deep mourning,

e. selective memory, when one experiences a fresh reminder of the loss, and

f. commitment to start living again.[7]

4. The way people experience loss shapes whether they suffer *anticipatory* grief, *sudden or traumatic* grief, *never-ending* grief, or *near-miss* grief.[8]

Pastoral theologians Kenneth Mitchell and Herbert Anderson offer additional perspectives in *All Our Losses, All Our Griefs*. Informed by the works of Bowlby and Kubler-Ross, they describe grief as "a particular response to the particular loss of a particular object."[9] No two experiences or expressions of grief are the same, as a wide range of feelings and various clusters of feelings—guilt, shame, loneliness, anxiety, anger, terror, bewilderment, emptiness, profound sadness, despair, helplessness—shape the way a person grieves.[10] Further, grief is shaped by the *intensity* of the attachment to the lost person or object, as well as by the *complexity* of this attachment.[11]

To Mitchell and Anderson, grief is multifaceted and contemplative, involving contemplation of the loss itself, the future without the lost person or object, and the feelings experienced within grief.[12] Common elements of grief include:

1. Numbness, as the loss represents a "shock" to the system.

2. Emptiness, loneliness, and isolation, each of which diminishes one's sense of self.

3. Fear and anxiety, given the dread of abandonment, the anxiety of separation, and fear of the future.
4. Guilt and shame, often consequences of regrets in the relationship or circumstances surrounding the loss.
5. Anger, which is equally powerful whether visible or unseen.
6. Sadness and despair.
7. Somatization, as powerful physiological symptoms emerge.[13]

Over the course of this process, the grieving person has multiple hopes:

♦ Hope that the deep feelings aroused by the loss will be acknowledged and expressed as fully as possible.
♦ Hope that one's attachments to the lost person or object, although not entirely relinquished, will be sufficiently altered that the grieving one may live with the reality of the loss and without constant reference to it.
♦ Hope that he or she will once again be able to make attachments to and investments in other people and things.
♦ Hope that his or her belief system, challenged and altered by the loss, will be restored.[14]

Still, grieving people may not be able to realize these hopes in the throes of a powerful grief because of their intolerance of pain, their need for control, or a lack of encouragement from others.[15]

Congregational leaders are wise to keep several concepts in mind. First, *leaders need to be sensitive to the sources and expressions of grief that will surface in their faith community.* As the previous two chapters have emphasized, there is an abundance of change, loss, and grief in congregational life and more specifically in the lives of individuals or groups of members. As leaders become more sensitive to the relationship of attachment to loss, they will understand more clearly why some people are grieving while others are not. This understanding should deepen their appreciation for the broken or breaking attachments grieving people have experienced.

Second, *congregational leaders must be mindful that grief is neither "clean" nor "linear."* However we frame the stages (or movements) of grief, we must remember that grieving is a messy, illogical process whose expression is marked by an array of intense feelings and whose complexity is based on our attachments to people or things lost and the circumstances surrounding the loss itself. There is no "map" for how people will grieve, no predictable timeline to indicate when the movements of grieving will be completed.

Sometimes people move through a period of numbness or shock and into a wide range of feelings—at times, conflicting emotions. As these become intense and overwhelming, people may begin to move back into numbness to counter their deep pain. Similarly, as people move toward an acceptance of loss and a time of reorganizing their lives, sadness or depression may pull them back to work through more painful feelings of loss.

Third, *congregational leaders need to remember that people grieve differently—in different ways and at different paces.* Typically, to understand how a person is grieving requires moving beyond familiar expressions of sympathy and focusing more intently on the nature of the attachment, the experience of the loss, and the responses of the grieving person to the broken or breaking attachment. To accompany one who grieves is to understand that a first experience of grieving, or *really* grieving, has its own challenges. It is to understand that those people who have previously grieved bring their experiences of loss and grief into the present grief. It is to understand that different personalities express grief differently. Some people grieve openly and outwardly, while others work through the loss and their feelings internally.

Fourth, *congregational leaders must understand that grieving people are "where they need to be."* We depreciate the grieving of people who are numb or in shock when we suggest that they need to "get over it" or when we attempt to spiritualize the loss so that they (or we) will feel better. When the intensity of loss is felt so deeply, the grieving person's best response, or defense, is to experience numbness—physically, emotionally, and spiritually—as he or she begins to come to grips with the reality of the loss. To attempt to lead people out of numbness or shock reflects a lack of respect for them and for their grief and speaks to our own discomfort with their loss and need to grieve.

Similarly, people need time and venues in which to express a variety of feelings, whether intense anger, deep sadness, guilt born of regret, or other feelings. Again, a leader's discomfort with such feelings may generate an impulse to help the person "move on" by accepting the loss and concluding (or at least concealing) the expressions of grief. Such impulses are not helpful.

Fifth, *congregational leaders must be aware that grief can be chaotic.* What has been normal is now lost, resulting in a degree of disorientation and disorganization in people's lives. Feeling disoriented, some people will express intense anger—not only because of the loss of the person or object to which they have been attached, but also because of the erosion of normality in their lives. Some people will yearn for the return of the lost person or object. Others will yearn for someone or something to replace what is lost, perhaps in an effort to reorient and reorganize their lives. And others will seek to re-establish control, whether in their own lives or in the lives of others.

Sixth, *congregational leaders need to be aware that for many people grieving is a significant "wilderness" experience.* Grieving people may feel alone, isolated, and uncertain of what the future holds. They may wonder whether they will survive. They may doubt themselves and vacillate between wanting and not wanting support. They may question God's goodness and presence. They may say they are not just experiencing loss but also feeling lost. They may feel hopeless. A person's time in such a wilderness may seem like forty years of endless grieving.

Finally, *congregational leaders must provide spiritual resources to grieving people.* People who are grieving may already possess some resources, although they have lost touch with them. Some resources are present in the faith community, which through its prayers and expressions of care may offer significant strength to the grieving person—strength offered not by "fixing" but by caring enough to stand with, to stand by, to listen, and to attempt to understand. Some resources present within both the grieving person and the faith community may be experienced and valued anew, especially the spiritual strength, comfort, and hope available through the presence of God.

A Pause to Reflect

Using the table on page 53, identify losses that have occurred in your congregation or that you anticipate. With each loss, identify people or groups that have had varying degrees of attachment to the loss. Identify the expressions of grief you perceive.

The Crucible of Anxiety

In times of change congregations, like individuals, experience and grieve loss. In grieving, congregations live between the pain of loss and the yearning of hope. And in the gap between grief and hope, congregations experience anxiety. In fact, it is within a crucible of anxiety that congregations move through grief, continuing to experience change as they (a) let go of people, places, and things to which they have been attached, and (b) find identities in new relationships. This section explores the sources and effects of anxiety in congregational life and strategies leaders may use to manage anxiety constructively.

Multiple sources of anxiety are present in congregational life. Many congregations feel less safe and secure than in the past. Gone are the days when they had comfortable cushions of financial, capital, and human assets. With diminishing

Losses— Actual or Anticipated	People or Groups with Significant Attachment— Evidence of Their Attachment	People or Groups with Moderate Attachment— Evidence of Their Attachment	Expressions of Grief by Various People or Groups

resources, congregations wonder whether they will survive. As uncertainty grows, so grows the pressure on pastors and other congregational leaders to respond to these problems and to inspire current and potential members. And often what people desire is a leader who will bring about renewal without change. As they eye narrowing margins of safety, many congregations become excessively dependent upon their leaders and form unrealistic expectations of what a pastor can do to "fix things." Many leaders—anxious themselves—buy into these dependencies and unrealistic expectations because they desire to be liked, accepted, and needed.

Congregations grieve because members and groups have lost significant defining points. Anxiety escalates as people sort through the realities of loss, their intense feelings, and the uncertainty of their future. And anxiety escalates further as a congregation and its leaders wonder how to (a) care for people who are grieving deeply, (b) respond to people who are grieving similar losses differently from each other, and (c) relate to people who are not grieving the changes at all because they feel no sense of loss. Pondering all the change, loss, and grief, leaders may become anxious about the congregation's undefined future and doubt whether its leaders have the necessary gifts to lead the congregation into unknown territory.

Multiple sources of anxiety create significant vulnerability for members, leaders, and congregations. This vulnerability fuels even more anxiety in the congregation, its leaders, and members.

If we understand anxiety as "energy that cannot sit still," then anxiety leads to movement. Karen Horney, a psychoanalyst who explored the nature and power of anxiety in the inner lives and outward relationships of people, identified three predominant strategies people use consciously or unconsciously to manage the energy of anxiety:

+ *Moving toward*: Some people adapt to the needs and expectations of others to diminish tension within the relationship. They often feel helpless as a result of anxiety and may become dependent upon others to avoid criticism, disapproval, or rejection.
+ *Moving away*: Some people avoid other people or situations that reinforce or intensify their anxiety. Pulling back, they often feel isolated as a result of anxiety and may become emotionally disengaged to protect themselves.
+ *Moving against*: Some people become argumentative, competitive, or defiant to reestablish their sense of control in

relation to others in whose presence they feel anxious. They often feel and express hostility and may give their desire for "power over another" higher priority than the quality of the relationship itself.[16]

Horney's frames of reference are helpful to congregational leaders and members as they seek to understand how anxiety affects people differently. When facing similar changes and losses, some members will become angry, if not hostile; others will disengage; others will "cozy up" to leaders. Regardless of the response, leaders must remember that each of the strategies people use is an expression of and a response to anxiety. Wise, effective leaders are sensitive to the differing responses of anxious members.

Just as individuals feel anxious, so do groups. British psychoanalyst Wilfred Bion observed that groups tend to function on two levels: as a *work group* and as a *basic assumption group*.[17] According to Bion, a work group functions on a rational level. As such, it pursues goals and objects, seeks harmony in working relationships, and learns from its positive and negative experiences. When a group is anxious, however, it may begin to function primarily on the basis of emotions, shifting from goal-oriented, rational, and conscious behavior to an emotional state driven by anxieties. In such situations, one or more patterns of group behavior, or basic assumptions, are likely to emerge:

- *Dependency*: A group undervalues what it has to offer in response to the challenges at hand and idealizes—or idolizes—a leader as the one who can resolve difficult situations and take care of people. The group's level of dependency, intensified by anxiety, becomes excessive, and no leader can fulfill the followers' unrealistic expectations for long.
- *Fight or flight*: A group believes that the only way it can preserve itself is through "fight" or "flight." Fighting may take aggressive forms, whether blaming, scapegoating, or threatening with words or behaviors. Flight may be

expressed by avoiding or withdrawing, or by ruminating on the past. Whatever the manifestation of anxiety, the underlying emotion is one of panic.

+ *Pairing*: A group looks to two of its members to create a solution, as if the birth of a new idea would save the group. Anticipation is a dominant feeling as members watch, wait, and hope that the pair will generate a new idea or an easy answer. Feelings of anger or despair begin to emerge when these hoped-for solutions are not quickly found.

While Horney's frames of reference help us understand the responses of individuals to anxiety, Bion encourages leaders to be attentive to how groups function when they are anxious. Congregational leaders are wise to notice these tendencies:

+ A group may be working on goal-oriented and emotional levels at the same time.

+ The emotional processes of a group may interfere with its capacity to progress toward its defined goals and objectives, intensifying the congregation's level of anxiety.

+ Subgroups within a congregation may concurrently exhibit the characteristics of different basic assumptions. For some subgroups, the emotional climate is one of excessive dependency; for others, one of aggression; for others, one of disengagement or withdrawal; and for still others, one of anticipation that when unfulfilled will lead to anger or despair.

+ Each subgroup has a different relationship with congregational leaders, different expectations of "effective" leadership, and different needs for its anxiety to be diminished.

+ Each subgroup has an impact upon leaders' comfort levels and capacities to lead as they deal with their own anxieties.

Finally, it is important to recognize that a congregation functions as a system when it experiences and responds to anxiety. More familiar to most congregational leaders than the theoretical frameworks of Karen Horney and Wilfred Bion is *family-systems theory,* which offers insight on a congregation's attempts to recover its sense of normality as it struggles with anxieties. Three concepts are key.[18]

1. *Homeostasis.* A congregation needs to remain "normal" by resisting changes that interfere with its functioning. Interruptions create a sense of imbalance within the faith community. The system itself and individuals and subgroups within it feel anxious and vulnerable when interference occurs, and the congregational system seeks to regain its balance.

2. *Triangulation.* When anxiety between two people or subgroups in a congregation creates a high level of discomfort in their relationship, they seek relief by discharging the anxiety. Consciously or unconsciously, they "triangulate"—they bring a third party (who often yearns to be helpful) into their relationship and attempt to use this outsider to diminish their level of anxiety. The creation of an "emotional triangle" affords the two people or subgroups a degree of relief. More often than not, the third party ends up feeling caught in the middle of the difficult relationship. Systemically, the congregation attempts to rebalance itself as the anxiety of the two is discharged onto the third and diffused into the system. These emotional triangles are common in anxious congregations—between two members and a lay leader; between two members and a pastor; between a member, a pastor, and a music director; among the staff. Sometimes the triangles seem endless.

Commonly the emergence of emotional triangles keeps a congregation and its parts stuck in anxious patterns. While discomfort between conflicted people or subgroups is alleviated, at least for a short period of time, the disturbance between them remains unresolved. Third parties generally experience a high degree of vulnerability as they are caught in the middle, feeling blamed, helpless, and used. When the third member is no longer a useful part of the triangle, the conflicted parties will seek and find another third member to help dispel or at least contain their anxiety.

3. *Identified patients.* It is common for anxious congregations to identify "difficult people" as the primary cause of their

problems or as significant roadblocks that prevent them from moving beyond the problems. By maintaining the focus on these identified people, congregational members and leaders can avoid identifying and responding to the real issues. When they perceive "identified patients" as roadblocks to change, their projections of blame and avoidance of responsibility prevent them from engaging in constructive and much-needed change. So while the identification of "difficult people" is intended to diminish systemic anxiety, it primarily reinforces the anxiety already present in the congregation.

Pastors, church staff members, lay leaders, members—any of these may be identified as a "difficult person." The identified patient's departure from a congregation characteristically leads to the identification of another difficult person to fill the role, creating an unending cycle unless leaders are able to end the scapegoating and redirect the attention from identified patients to the congregation as a system.

Horney, Bion, and family systems theory all make clear that the sources of anxiety in congregational life are complex and the effect of anxiety is powerful. When faith communities endure change, loss, and grief, how might leaders help individuals and groups manage anxiety constructively?

First, *leaders must seek to understand as clearly as possible the sources and effects of anxiety in the congregations*. I hope the perspectives offered in this section provide conceptual frameworks that will help leaders identify the presence and impact of anxiety.

Second, *leaders must understand that anxiety is a response to a threat*. As such, it is a complex mixture of anger and fear, with differing degrees of fear and anger for various people. It is insufficient to attempt to counter or contain the anxiety that surfaces in a congregation. The key to dismantling the anxiety is identifying and responding to the underlying threat. A primary threat in congregational life centers on change and loss, particularly in relation to people, places, and things to which attachments have been strong.

Third, *leaders must understand that unmanaged anxiety diminishes the capacity of congregations to respond creatively and boldly to losses and challenges.* The more congregations are oriented to survival and the more readily they seek quick and painless solutions, the less they embody the flexibility and resilience needed to learn new things and to become new creatures.

Fourth, *leaders must understand that anxiety, as energy, creates pressure in the life of a faith community.* Metaphorically, a congregation is a vessel—perhaps a pressure cooker—in which the energy and intensity of anxiety grow.[19]

This image of a pressure cooker reminds me of childhood visits to my grandmother's house. Coming in through the screened-in back porch for dinner, I knew immediately when she was cooking butter beans in the pressure cooker. I could smell the beans cooking and hear the hiss of the pressure cooker as the valve was loosened to alleviate some—but not all—of the pressure.

Two variables, it seems, are crucial for managing energy in a pressure cooker—the amount of heat and the capacity of the valve to relieve pressure. Without heat and pressure, there's no energy, no possibility for change. But with too much heat and pressure, the cooker may explode, making a mess of the kitchen.

Leaders are wise to understand that managing anxiety constructively requires attentiveness to the "heat" and the "pressure valve" as congregational anxiety intensifies. Perhaps keeping one hand on the heat regulator and the other on the pressure valve can help leaders use anxiety to bring about hopeful change.

Finally, *leaders must maintain healthy relationships with each other and with members of the congregation if they are to be effective.* As anxiety rises, leaders must themselves be healthy if they are to nurture the health and well-being of a congregation—healthy as individuals; healthy in their patterns of relating to others; healthy in their awareness of what they can and cannot do alone; and healthy in managing their own anxieties in the face of change, loss, and grief.

A Pause to Reflect

Reflect upon and discuss with other leaders your responses to the following questions:

1. What do you perceive to be the most significant sources of anxiety in your congregation?
2. Several conceptual frameworks have been offered to stimulate your thinking and to deepen your awareness about the effects of anxiety.
   a. Which seem most relevant to your congregation at this time?
   b. With these frameworks in mind, how do you assess relationships among members? Among leaders? Between members and leaders?
3. What options might you and other leaders pursue to manage anxiety constructively in the congregation?

Developing the Capacity to Attach Anew

In an introductory course in pastoral care during my first year of seminary, I was introduced to common conceptual frameworks for understanding grief. Here is what I remember:

+ Initially, grieving people experience shock, numbness, and denial to counter the pain of loss.
+ Subsequently, grieving people experience a variety of feelings, their depth depending on the circumstances surrounding the loss. Such feelings, including sadness and anger, and the depression to which they can lead, may become so

strong that people revert to shock and numbness. In other words, grief is not linear and neatly sequential.

♦ Potentially, grieving people come to accept the reality of loss. With such acceptance, their grief comes to an end.

From my work with attachment theorists, I have come to appreciate a dimension beyond acceptance that provides a deeper fulfillment to grieving people. I refer to this as *attaching anew*. Foundational to this concept is the principle that *attaching anew* is not the same as reattaching. Furthermore, developing the capacity to attach anew requires hard work.

Reattachment implies that it is somehow possible to re-establish a connection to what has been lost but no longer exists. Clearly, the possibility of reattaching is tantalizing to grieving people and congregations. Reattachment would restore broken bonds and lost relationships. Reattaching would terminate the intense feelings of sadness and anger, fear and despair. Reattaching would allow congregational members and leaders to avoid the expressions of anxiety that disrupt relationships and distract the congregation from its ministries. Reattaching would allow us to return to the stability we enjoyed in the past. In sum, it would halt the grief that displaces, at least for some time, the hope that inspires and shapes our ministry.

But it is not possible to reattach to what is lost and gone. Despite a desire to cling to precious memories, despite heartfelt yearnings for leadership that will restore these broken bonds and relationships of the past, we cannot reattach to what is lost. It is gone, and in our grieving we must let it go to move into the future.

What is possible is that congregational leaders and members can attach anew. To do so, *they must thoroughly grieve the losses that one, many, or all have experienced.* Members who are not grieving a particular change (or loss) must understand that other people *are* grieving, and members must support them, pray for them, express a heartfelt concern, and give them sufficient time to grieve. To shortchange grief is to rush people to a false sense of acceptance. Surely this haste diminishes their ability to accept the reality and finality of the loss and blocks their capacity to attach anew.

Second, *congregational members and leaders must learn to exercise restraint as anxiety arises.* In times of grieving, the emotional climate of a congregation may be one of free-floating anxiety. We may view others' words and behaviors through the lenses of anxiety, which will distort communication between people and disfigure treasured relationships. Members and leaders may personalize remarks that are not personal, escalating the pain. Acquiring the ability to identify multiple sources and effects of anxiety makes it possible to exercise restraint as it emerges.

Third, *congregational members and leaders must realize that their temptation to reattach is born of several factors beyond the broken or breaking relationship with an important person, place, or thing.* Members may yearn to reattach because they fear that the congregation will never experience such vitality again, that it will continue to decline, and that eventually it will die. Conversely, they may fear that the congregation will change so much that it will no longer be the faith community they have known and loved, and in which they have invested themselves so deeply—that the traditions of the congregation will be lost or marginalized as it moves into the future. In either case, they fear additional losses at a time when they are already grieving.

Fourth, *leaders and members must understand the importance of honoring and preserving the best of the past as the congregation addresses the future.* Amid losses, it is easier to accept the finality of loss and to attach anew when visible lines of continuity connect where the congregation has been and where it may be going.

Fifth, *leaders and members must attend to relationships within the congregation, affirming the centrality of healthy relationships if congregations are to become and remain healthy.* In the midst of loss and grief and the frustration of anxiety, it is easy for leaders and members to lose some or much of the trust they have extended to each other. Breaking or broken trust diminishes the capacity of people to grieve together or beside each other, to remain hopeful about the future of their congregation, and to attach anew.

Sixth, *congregational leaders and members must comprehend that the capacity to attach anew is born of faith and inspired by hope.* Rather than attempting to reattach themselves to what is lost and gone, they appreciate that attaching anew is an expression of hope and a manifestation of confidence in the future. They appreciate that hope and confidence are expressions of faith in one another, the congregation, and God's hand amid loss, grief, and anxiety. As members and leaders grow in faith, hope, and confidence, they trust that new possibilities await them and trust that God will continue to lead the congregation, inspiring it and calling it to respond in faith. At its best, the congregation understands that to attach anew is to experience resurrection.

Finally, *leaders and members appreciate the role of vision as they invest in a future that is promised and being fulfilled.* Vision functions as a bridge from the past to the future. Just as vision allows us to see with some clarity what has come before us and what dimensions of our past we value, vision also allows us to see into the future, even if dimly. With vision, as it relates to both the past and the future, we are able to grieve as those who have hope.

Beyond the Pain of Change

In helping congregations name and grieve their losses, live in the crucible of anxiety, and develop the capacity to *attach anew*, pastors and other leaders serve as "stewards" as people grieve. As they do so, effective leaders typically see themselves playing multiple roles in congregational life:

- As "stabilizers" for members experiencing loss and grief, and attaching anew.
- As "friends" to some and "foes" to others, as they make important and sometimes difficult decisions in the process of change.
- As "sources of inspiration" to those desiring to follow their lead.

Leadership is never easy. As congregations learn to embrace change, leaders guide them toward what will be. As congregations seek to develop or refine a vision of the future, leaders assist members struggling to attach anew. As congregations move in new directions, as exciting and uncertain as these may be, leaders make, or lead the congregation in making, many choices—about which directions to pursue first, which needs to respond to, how to allocate limited resources when needs exceed resources. And that is when leadership becomes real.

For Reflection and Discussion

1. What is most exciting to you as you reflect upon the capacity of your congregation to *attach anew*?
2. What concerns you?

CHAPTER FOUR

The Power of Vision to Embrace Change

I had always thought I had perfect vision—or at least near-perfect vision. As an adolescent I sometimes "manipulated" my eyes a little during eye examinations to read the 20/20 line on the eye chart. Corrective lenses? I wanted nothing to do with them. Perhaps this reluctance was vanity, or simply a desire not to be encumbered with glasses.

During a visit to an ophthalmologist during my second year of seminary, the diagnosis was clear: I needed corrective lenses. I vividly remember putting on my glasses for the first time. Walking out of the doctor's office, I looked at the grass, at the leaves on the trees, at the clouds in the sky. The colors were vivid, the details sharp. By alternately removing the glasses and putting them back on, I could see major contrasts. I did this several times as I looked around. With these new lenses, I could see things in a way different from before. I had no clue what I was missing until I began to wear corrective lenses.

In the first three chapters, I offered several sets of lenses in the hope that they will assist congregational leaders and members to see in a new and different way—lenses related to attachment, change, and loss; lenses related to anxiety and grief; lenses related to the hope of attaching anew.

This chapter focuses on vision—more specifically, on the role of vision for congregations struggling to attach anew as they move toward a largely undefined future. Three components shape this chapter:

+ The critical place of vision in congregational life.
+ Impediments to vision in many congregations.
+ The power of vision to embrace change.

The Critical Place of Vision in Congregational Life

"Where there is no vision, the people perish" (Prov. 29:18a, KJV). This citation is popular for congregations seeking to cast a vision, or to follow one. More contemporary translations render this passage differently. In the New Revised Standard Version we read: "Where there is no prophecy, the people cast off restraint." In the New International Version: "Where there is no revelation, the people cast off restraint." In the Revised English Bible: "With no one in authority, the people throw off all restraint." In the Berkeley Version: "Where there is no vision the people run wild."

Clearly, vision is vital as we seek to find our way—or to stay the course. In some translations, vision allows for life, perhaps vitality; and to be without vision is to perish. In other translations, vision does not come from within us but is given to us by an external source of authority, whether as prophecy or revelation. Such vision seemingly stimulates us to some form of action and prevents us from "running wild."

In considering the nuances of these translations, many congregational members and leaders may not see how the passage relates to their situation. While they may be struggling, they are not yet concerned that they will perish. While levels of anxiety may escalate in times of change, loss, and grief, there is little fear that members and leaders will "run wild"— or even cast off restraint. A seminary colleague has proposed that the passage suggests that where there is no vision, the people *flounder*. Now, that's an image with which many congregations may resonate! Amid change, and the loss and grief that accompany change, many congregations find themselves floundering as they try to set a course for the future and figure out how and to what they might attach anew.

Vision is a key factor in how congregations embrace change, move beyond the intense pain of loss, and rediscover their capacity to hope. Congregations that remain in the grip of loss and grief and anxiety and are unable to see the present clearly—or to envision the future—are likely to flounder, and eventually to perish.

A Pause to Reflect

1. What visions does your congregation have of its future?
2. What visions do you and other church leaders have of your congregation in the future?
3. How much is your congregation floundering at this time? What signs of floundering do you see?

Impediments to Vision in Congregations

From my work with congregations and leaders, and my reading of leadership theorists on discernment, vision, and strategic planning, it is clear to me that many congregations face significant impediments to finding their "vision." These impediments may generate or reinforce congregational floundering, prevent congregations from engaging in "visioning work," and diminish the capacity of members and leaders to attach anew.

Impediment 1

We are not clear what we mean by "vision." Many congregational members and leaders are ambivalent about the nature and purpose of "vision" in congregational life. Does "vision" refer to a *capacity to see?* Does it mean the capacity *to see what is ahead?* Or the capacity *to define what is ahead?* To the degree that congregational members and leaders remain confused about what "vision" implies, they will flounder.

As congregations begin to craft a vision for future ministry, leaders must help them clarify several aspects of a "good" vision. Effective leaders enable congregations to see with clarity:

- What is behind them—not only the facts of their history, but more important, (a) the ways their history and traditions have shaped them, (b) the ways previous members and leaders have inspired them, (c) the strengths they have enjoyed, (d) the challenges they have faced, and (e) the changes they have endured.
- What is ahead—the opportunities, challenges, and choices before them as they imagine what it will mean to be (or to become) a vital faith community.
- What is around them—the contexts in which they live and serve, including the gifts and needs of their neighbors near and far.
- What is beneath them—their foundations for ministry, the rock upon which they stand.
- What is above them—God, who creates, redeems, and sustains, and whose transformative grace provides a vision under which their visions are cast.

Impediment 2

We are uncertain who takes the first step in casting a vision. Vision must begin with someone, whether an individual or a group. Understandably, congregations turn to their leaders as the initiators of vision, hoping that they will cast a vision that will at least "fix" the problems the congregation is facing and inspire members to join the effort. More often than not, lay leaders look to one or two from their number or to their pastor to take the first step in casting a vision.

When congregations are struggling with change and the stakes are high as they look to the future, leaders may hesitate to take that first step in casting a vision. They are aware of members' heightened expectations, some of which are unrealistic. They are aware that grieving members look to them to ease pain. They feel pressure from members who yearn for a clearly defined "map" to alleviate fears. Leaders may be tempted to defer to one another to take the first step. However, someone must take the initiative if the congregation is to cast a vision. Otherwise, it will remain stuck and continue to flounder.

In a recent devotion on our seminary campus, a pastor suggested that *hope hears the music of the future—and faith dances to it.* This statement reminds leaders that they must have hope to have vision. They must have faith to be inspired by the music and begin to dance to it. Someone must be willing to take that first dance step, however awkward, if the congregation is to learn to move to the music.

In many congregations, the pastor fulfills the role of helping other leaders listen to the music and take the first steps in casting a vision. This is not to imply that casting a vision is a pastor's role. That responsibility usually belongs to the leadership team.

Impediment 3

We are not clear about the purpose of congregational participation in casting a vision. Congregations are often unclear about how members can be constructively involved in vision casting. As a result, leaders and members often make two strategic errors in "listening processes."

First, congregational leaders often describe members as "stakeholders" in the process. While leaders intend to emphasize the importance of listening to members to respond to their needs and increase their ultimate ownership of the vision, calling members stakeholders is unwise. Stakeholders will retain their "stake" so long as they believe they are receiving appropriate returns on their investments. When their dividends disappoint them, they are apt to withdraw their stake and to reinvest it in another vehicle that may pay more satisfactory returns. Such an image of congregational life reinforces our culture's consumerist and individualistic values and diminishes members' identity as disciples who participate in the church's ministry to give and to serve, not to receive and reinvest. To be sure, in listening processes, leaders must listen carefully to members. But the aim of listening is not to inspire members to hold a stake in the church but to inspire them to grow in their faith and practice as disciples of Jesus Christ.

Second, members may have unrealistic expectations of how leaders will use their ideas in casting a vision. More than once, I have heard powerful members critique church leaders for not listening to what they have said—angry that church leaders asked for but did not incorporate their input. Leaders who really listened to them, they insist, would shape the vision in accordance with their suggestions.

As congregational leaders consider ways to solicit and make use of congregational input, I offer three suggestions. First, leaders should use listening processes to learn more about their congregations as members share experiences, ideas, and feelings. Second, leaders should replace *stakeholder* imagery with the language of *discipleship.* Ultimately, members will develop a much deeper sense of ownership of visions that adhere faithfully to the gospel, inspire them to serve God and neighbor, and assist them in developing their religious faith and practice. Third, leaders should invite members to share their hopes, dreams, and visions—and remind them that these, along with the hopes, dreams, and visions of others, will serve as a basis upon which a vision is cast.

Impediment 4

Leaders wonder whether members own the vision. The issue of ownership is one of the most challenging impediments that congregations must overcome in casting and realizing a vision. After all, a vision without buy-in is like a bridge to nowhere.

Congregational leaders must assess the degree to which members accept an emerging vision. First, they must understand that ownership of a vision is not the same as verbal assent to it. Too often, leaders believe that members have "accepted" a vision because they have not opposed it. As leaders move to develop and activate objectives and plans to fulfill the vision, they may quickly become aware that the congregation does not *really* support the vision and the changes it represents. Before moving ahead, leaders must test the pulse of members to determine their true support of, or resistance to, an emerging vision.

Second, leaders must understand that different degrees of ownership are required for different visions. With some visions, ownership by 30 percent of the congregation is adequate to ensure that the vision is enacted—depending on which 30 percent buys in. With other visions, even 90 percent is inadequate. And in some congregations, it takes only one or two powerful voices to thwart a vision, regardless of how enthusiastic the rest of the congregation is. Accordingly, leaders may want to consider the following questions:

+ What degree of ownership is required for the vision to be enacted?
+ How will we know whether members are buying in to the vision?
+ Do a few members or subgroups within the congregation have the power to thwart the vision? If so, how might we proceed with the vision and these members or subgroups?
+ What steps might we take to build more ownership for the vision?

Impediment 5

Leaders have not considered to what degree the vision should relate to the past. Clearly, vision points to what the future may hold. The process of casting a vision may be creative and hopeful and provide a source of considerable energy and enthusiasm as a congregation considers future ministry opportunities. The most effective "visioning processes" typically look forward *and backward*, learning from the past without being restricted by it.

Some leaders ignore the congregation's rich past in casting a vision. Hoping to move boldly into the future, they may overlook the voices and traditions of the past and proceed too quickly with new initiatives. In doing so, they place the congregation at risk—and their capacity for effective leadership in peril.

Strategic leaders seek to cast a vision that builds upon the best of the past as a congregation moves toward the future. They understand that a degree of continuity with the past allows members to "connect the dots" between past, emerging, and future realities. They know that appropriating the past diminishes unnecessary risks and enables "measured" change. They are sensitive to the negative impact of discontinuities between the vision and the past and recognize that the greater the dissonance, the more likely it is that members attached to the past will resist the vision.

Yet strategic leaders are equally aware of the dangers of remaining fixed on the past and avoiding the difficult task of casting a vision. Staying focused on the past may reflect a wish to relive it. Further, it is to miss emerging opportunities for ministry on the congregation's doorstep or on the other side of the world.

Congregations must find a balance between the past and the future in the casting of a vision. Failure to determine an appropriate balance is one of the challenges leaders face in vision casting and an impediment that leads many congregations to avoid the difficult work of engaging each other in casting a vision.

Impediment 6

Leaders are unaware of the power of unresolved grief. The two previous chapters focused extensively on grief. In sum, congregations in which members and subgroups are grieving unresolved losses—where numbness, deep sadness, anger, and anxiety persist—have a diminished capacity to attach anew. These grieving people are not yet able to envision a future, much less to commit themselves to visions that others have cast. To move forward too quickly with vision casting is to leave some or many behind. Those left behind will not only resist the vision—they also will resent those leaders and members who have moved ahead without them.

Strategic leaders are aware, however, that they cannot wait until everyone is finished grieving before the congregation casts a vision for the future. To do so would immobilize a congregation and generate a high degree of passivity and inactivity. To overcome this impediment, leaders must assess the presence and power of unresolved grief and determine when it is time to move forward—with the knowledge that some members will not support them or the new vision.

Impediment 7

The envisioned pace of change is too fast or too slow. Pacing is critical. Equally critical is leaders' awareness that while the rate of change for some people may be too fast, for others that rate may be too slow. Consequently, it may be tempting not to move at all. At least leaders will not be criticized for the pace of change. (Of course, they may be criticized for doing nothing at all.)

To set an appropriate pace of change, leaders should consider the following strategies:

+ If the vision might involve a significant degree of change, listen carefully to the congregational traditions of the past. Seek to resurrect certain traditions that may contribute to the fulfillment of the vision. After all, the bolder the vision, the more it needs to be connected to the past as leaders attempt to manage the pace of change.

+ Consider small yet significant steps when embracing change. These steps will allow for a pace of change that does not exceed the congregation's capacity to tolerate the difficulties of change. Moreover, these steps will build confidence in the future and generate positive momentum that builds a congregation's true ownership of the emerging vision.

+ Consider the pace of change in relation to available resources. Too often, congregational visions are lofty, out of touch with the available human, financial, and capital resources. Without necessary resources to support change, the vision is likely to collapse. Congregations and leaders will carry the scars of the failed vision and will lack sufficient trust in each other to envision together again for a long time.

Impediment 8

We feel pressure to guarantee the "perfect" vision. In the face of change, congregational members and leaders want to find the "perfect" vision. An imperfect vision, they fear, will not be successful and will lead to more loss. In the face of the losses the congregation has already endured, the stakes are too high for the congregation to get it wrong. The pressures to cast a perfect vision, I fear, keep congregational leaders and members from engaging in a visioning process that is bold, creative, and ultimately life-giving.

Congregational leaders cannot guarantee the perfect vision. What leaders can do is to underscore the importance of casting a vision that encourages the vitality of the congregation and the purposefulness of its ministry.

Impediment 9

Leaders think a vision statement can include the preferences of all congregational members and leaders. Members and leaders aspire to craft a vision statement that will be "owned" by all people in the congregation. Clearly, this is a challenging dimension of a visioning process. Inevitably, some members will feel marginalized and angry when they perceive that the unfolding vision is incompatible with their own vision for the congregation. How can a vision statement be a vision statement for all, given the diversity of the congregation and the various hopes, needs, and priorities of its members and leaders? Whose vision will be expressed as the congregation's vision of the future—and what does the outcome mean for members and leaders who feel left out or left behind?

Aware of diverse hopes, needs, and priorities, leaders sometimes differ over how to synthesize the visions of the congregation into a coherent statement. Some are tempted to create a vision statement that reflects the majority, or at least the majority of the most active members, aware that no single statement will satisfy all. Others are tempted to cast a series of vision statements: they hope that the inclusion of each will reflect the diversity of the congregation and mollify the members, and they trust that the relation of each vision statement to the overall mission of the church will create enough cohesion to allow the congregation to maintain its unity. In most cases, this strategy delays the allocation of limited financial, capital, and human assets until leaders determine how to raise and allocate resources for these visionary emphases.

Impediment 10

Our vision does not inspire the hearts of people. Visioning processes and the visions they produce often fail to inspire members and leaders. In strategic planning processes, congregations may subordinate their "vision" to concrete objectives, intended outcomes, assigned responsibilities, and detailed timelines. Aware of the pressure to grow by attracting new members, for example, many leaders focus their attention on action plans to address immediate needs. Accordingly, they neglect to attend to the vision that would inspire people to respond, to catalyze these strategies, and to move into a promising future. To be sure, they may craft a vision statement. Yet in my experience with congregations, this vision statement is almost inevitably the weakest part of their strategic planning.

Second, the process of casting a vision is generally so analytical that the vision fails to speak to the heart. People need to be "moved" if they are to change. As convincing as thoughtful visioning processes and statements may be, they are unlikely to prove effective if they do not touch the hearts of members, especially those who have been grieving. If people are to connect to the vision, their hearts must be re-engaged. Accordingly, leaders are wise to consider well-conceived plans making use of stories, rituals, and symbols that inspire the hearts of people.

Finally, and most important, a congregation's vision must reflect God's vision for the church and world if it is to capture the imaginations of members and leaders. At their best, congregational leaders may become adept at engaging congregational resources and perspectives in the casting of a vision. They may effectively build consensus for change as they integrate perspectives from the past and present and from leaders and members.

What leaders often do not do well is to consider God's vision for the congregation. To be sure, they may frame their work as a "discernment" process. Yet, their intent may be to discern what the members want (and will follow) rather than to discern what God hopes and what mission God is calling them toward. Aligning a congregation's vision with God's vision for the church and world is a congregation's best chance of inspiring the hearts of people. And it is the most faithful.

Remember the proverb: *Where there is no vision, the people flounder.* The second part of this verse says, *But happy are those who keep the law* (NRSV). Congregational members and leaders are wise to see that it is our relationship to God and our alignment to God's vision that inspire the hearts of people and allow us to find our way.

For Reflection and Discussion

Answer, as honestly as possible, the following questions in relation to your congregation. Discuss your responses with other leaders and compare the similarities and differences in your responses.

1. What do we mean by "vision"?
2. Who will take the first step in casting a vision?
3. What is the purpose of congregational participation in casting a vision?
4. How much ownership does our congregation have in the vision?
5. To what degree should the vision relate to the past?
6. How much unresolved grief remains, and what is its power?
7. Is the pace of change envisioned for our congregation too fast or too slow?
8. How might we counter pressure to cast a "perfect" vision?
9. How might we seek broad ownership of a vision statement that cannot include the preferences of all congregational members and leaders?
10. How might our vision inspire the hearts of people?

The Power of Vision to Embrace Change

Casting a vision is hard work. The leader who rises to the challenge to cast a vision that truly inspires a congregation empowers members to embrace change. Wise leaders understand that the power of vision stems more from the vision itself than from the visionary. Further, they realize that an inspiring vision mobilizes congregations to work through substantial challenges and to make significant choices as they seek a future to which members will attach anew.

The power of vision is evident to me as I write this section. The board of trustees at the seminary where I teach recently adopted a new strategic plan for 2009–2014. Like many strategic plans, our plan bears the following structure:

- Our mission statement.
- A description of our mission and purpose. Some people would view this description as an identity statement, as it links key attributes of our seminary to our core mission.
- A theology for vision.
- Objectives of our strategic plan in twelve areas of our seminary's life and work.
- A glimpse into the future after 2014.
- A theology for action.

This plan is twenty-three pages long. It evolved over eighteen months and many drafts and revisions. It required hard work involving many people, and it represented important work for the seminary in its service to the church for which we prepare leaders.

What impresses me the most about our strategic plan is its *theology for vision*. This two-page statement "sings." Bearing the fingerprints of our seminary president, it begins with an affirmation that the future, like the past and present, belongs to God. It specifies our task not as defining the future so much as comprehending how God is forming the future in a way that invites us to respond faithfully and freely to God's movement in the world.

Central to this theology for vision is its emphasis on the reign of God in the life, death, and resurrection of Jesus, in the extent of his lordship, and in the church's call to represent

Jesus. As a teaching institution of the church, our seminary seeks to bear witness to the reign of God in our stewardship of resources.

The objectives of our strategic plan follow our theology of vision—our planning follows our vision. Faced with shrinking financial assets, our seminary is unable to sustain all its programs of the past. We must become more focused and use our precious resources more wisely. For the foreseeable future, we will have a smaller faculty and staff, a smaller physical plant, and fewer degree programs. Difficult decisions are being made in the face of painful reductions.

Despite the pain, however, new sources of energy are evident. To some, this energy comes from a sharper focus in the relation of our programs and activities to our mission. To others, this energy comes from the strategic plan's emphasis on strengthening the orientation of our seminary to the needs of congregational leaders for leadership development. To me, this energy comes from the inspiring power of our vision. We are celebrating the reign of God. Its continuing transformation of the church and seminary is empowering us to embrace change even as we make difficult and painful decisions.

For Reflection and Discussion

1. What biblical themes are central to your congregation?
2. How might these themes shape your theology of vision for the future?
3. In what ways might a focused theology of vision empower your congregation to make important decisions in the future?

A New Vision, A New Way

What could energize a congregation more than a vision for its future that is focused in Scripture, relevant to its historical and contemporary contexts, and faithful in its service to God in the future? An inspiring vision enables us to see beyond the painful losses and overwhelming challenges that have caused us to flounder; it prepares us to find a new way.

Wise leaders understand that vision provides a crucial source of power for embracing change. Vision by itself, however, is insufficient. Leaders must be adept at linking a vision to key attributes of the congregation's identity.

Chapter 5 explores how leaders may discover a vision in existing congregational values and stories. This is not as easy as it sounds, because a new vision also points toward *emerging* values and ministries. Differing visions for the future will come into view as members and leaders embrace existing and emerging values, stories, and ministries. Leaders must decide how to proceed in casting a vision that will focus precious resources for ministry.

CHAPTER FIVE

The Discovery of Vision in Values and Stories

Where do we go from here? Congregational leaders face this question regularly as they attempt to figure out how to chart a course for the future. At their best, they clearly understand the dynamics of loss and change, the processes of grieving, the importance of attaching anew, and the power of vision to embrace change. What these leaders struggle with is how to move forward into uncharted territory.

Three critical tasks await leaders who seek new directions for their congregations:

+ Task 1: Finding vision in *existing* values and stories
+ Task 2: Finding vision in *emerging* values and stories
+ Task 3: Finding vision in *God's* values and stories

This chapter strives to equip leaders for the critical task of setting a course for the future—a course that will enable the congregation to experience new sources of energy and a deeper sense of vitality as members seek to love and serve God and neighbor.

Task 1: Finding Vision
in Existing Values and Stories

One of the most commonly used strategies for discovering vision for the future is identifying a congregation's existing values. Leaders anticipate that if they can distill a congregation's core values, a vision will emerge that inspires the congregation to embrace change and move forward.

Leaders tend to choose one of two approaches for identifying existing values in a congregation. Most often, they attempt to select attractive words that describe how the congregation sees itself, or wants to—words like biblical, traditional, authentic, safe, contemporary, open, affirming, hospitable, Spirit-led, missional, and joyful. These values may provide a significant basis for the discovery of a vision for the future. For some members, however, words alone lack the power to inspire new actions.

Other leaders use a different approach to identify existing values. Instead of selecting descriptive words, they look for past and contemporary stories that exhibit the congregation's values. These accounts may embody the leadership of previous pastors and staff members, the faithful service of long-time Sunday school teachers, the insights from retreats and mission trips, and the joy of Christmas pageants involving children of the congregation and community. Within these stories, leaders may see the values mentioned above. Linked to congregational stories, these values become more inspiring to many members.

The first task for leaders who seek a new direction for their congregations is to uncover vision in existing *values and stories*. This task will take the conversations about the future back to the past and will entail remembering the joyful moments and painful losses identified in chapter 2—memories of former members and staff, the congregation's central place in members' lives, some of the congregation's most deeply held traditions, and structural supports for congregational life that no longer exist. The purpose of this task is not to reopen grieving processes or to recreate the past. Rather it is intended to:

♦ Identify values that are deep in the history of the congregation and central to its present identity.

♦ Draw upon the wisdom of the past as the congregation discovers a vision for the future.

♦ Tap into an important source of energy in people for whom the past offers inspiration.

♦ Deepen the cohesion of the congregation by linking existing and emerging values in congregational stories.

For Reflection and Discussion

1. What existing values epitomize *core* dimensions of your congregation's identity?

2. Identity three past or contemporary stories that capture the essence of your congregation. Why did you select these stories?

3. What values are embedded in these three stories? How do these values compare with the core values you identified above?

Task 2: Finding Vision in Emerging Values and Stories

Effective leaders realize that a vision for the future is often embedded in values and stories that are only beginning to emerge. Because of the emerging dimension of these values and stories, leaders are asked to *see around the curve*, anticipating what may be coming without any assurance that it will materialize.

How can leaders discover vision in emerging values and stories? I suggest that they begin to search for *narratives of aspiration*.[1] These narratives represent leaders' hopes for their congregations as they strike out in new directions and provide a significant basis for a vision of the future. Narratives of aspiration are seen in congregations where leaders and members envision:

- A congregation that experiences a renewed sense of vitality as a Christian community, discovers a deepened relationship with God, and develops new ministries in which members' gifts are shared in the community.
- A congregation whose membership is shrinking, whose leaders are making difficult choices about which ministries to continue, and where new sources of energy are emerging as priorities become more focused.
- A sanctuary remodeled to embody a more contemporary and versatile style, so that this space may be used for worship, education, and fellowship.
- More training of lay leaders to broaden the congregation's emphasis on education, mission, and outreach.
- New partnerships with other congregations to respond more generously and effectively to hunger and homelessness within the community.

The *second task* for leaders who seek a new direction for their congregations is to uncover vision in emerging values and stories. I believe this happens naturally, beginning with stories, since people are curious about how a story will unfold. As leaders begin to see emerging stories in their congregation's life, they can look for the emerging values embedded in these stories. Consider the examples from above:

- A congregation that experiences a renewed sense of vitality as a Christian community, discovers a deepened relationship with God, and develops new ministries in which members' gifts are shared in the community: An emerging value may be *an increased emphasis on personal and congregational discipleship* that expresses love for God and neighbor.
- A congregation that is losing members, whose leaders are making difficult choices about which ministries to continue,

and where new sources of energy are emerging as priorities become more focused: An emerging value may be *a deeper appreciation of congregational ministries* that are most precious to members, leaders, and the community.

+ A worship space renovated to serve more contemporary and versatile functions, so that it may be used for worship, education, and fellowship: An emerging value may be *a stewardship of space* that affirms the sanctuary's centrality for worship while making it more accessible for multiple uses appropriate to the congregation's ministries.

+ More training of lay leaders to broaden the congregation's emphasis on education, mission, and outreach: An emerging value may be *the empowerment of more people* to participate energetically in the congregation's ministries.

+ New partnerships with other congregations to respond more generously and effectively to hunger and homelessness within the community: An emerging value may be *the desire to work more collaboratively with neighboring congregations* to respond to fundamental human needs in the community.

Emerging stories, however, are not the only places where leaders may find new directions. Fresh ideas may surface also in emerging changes in the community surrounding the congregation. Consider three dimensions of change that are having a significant impact on communities and new directions the congregation might pursue:

+ *Emerging technologies*: How might a congregation use the Internet as an opportunity for evangelism, a tool for congregational communication, and a mechanism for making the resources of Christian faith and practice more available to members and nonmembers? How might a pastor use Facebook, Twitter, or text messaging to build relationships with youth and young adults?

+ *Economic crises*: How might a congregation provide support for members and nonmembers whose lives have been significantly affected by the recent economic crisis? How might congregational leaders create networking groups, help others redevelop their resumes, and work with other people in the community to strengthen emergency assistance programs?

+ *Immigrant groups*: How might a congregation reach out to diverse immigrant groups in communities and neighborhoods? How might members assist adults with English-speaking skills? How might members offer tutoring to children and youth who are struggling with schoolwork? How might the congregation provide appropriate space for immigrant congregations that are looking for a place to worship?

In each of these areas, imagine the impact on the energy of your members and the vitality of your congregation if it responds to emerging opportunities for ministry. Each of these examples points toward the possibility of realizing emerging stories, based on emerging values. But to move toward these possibilities, leaders must *see around the curve*.

For Reflection and Discussion

1. What changes do you observe in your congregation? How might these changes shape your future ministry?
2. What changes do you observe in your community? What new opportunities might your congregation pursue in response to these changes?
3. What emerging stories do you envision in anticipation of the future? How could these stories strengthen your congregation's ministry?
4. What emerging values do you see within these stories? How might these values inspire new sources of energy and a deeper sense of vitality for your congregation?

Task 3: Finding Vision in God's Values and Stories

The previous chapter cited the proverb "Where there is no vision, the people flounder [perish]. But happy are those who keep the law" (Prov. 29:18). This proverb suggests that congregational leaders are wise to see that our relationship to God and our alignment to God's vision inspire the hearts of people and allow us to find our way.

Finding vision in existing congregational values and stories is an important task of leadership. Similarly, leaders must discover vision in emerging values and stories. But completing these two tasks alone is insufficient to guide a congregation into the future. The *third task* is critical: leaders must find vision in God's values and stories. How leaders are able to complete this task is less clear to them, and their confidence wanes as they struggle with how to proceed faithfully.

I suggest that leaders proceed in three areas as they attempt to find vision in God's values and stories. This course of action reflects a process of discernment that takes seriously the relation of our values and stories to God's values and stories.

Scriptural Stories

Congregational leaders are wise to invest time alone and together in the study of Scripture to continue in their journey of discipleship and to deepen their capacity for faithful leadership. In scriptural texts, leaders find stories of God's continuing activity among people—activity that works toward the redemption of all creation. In these stories, leaders observe people of faith struggling with change and looking for leadership among kings and prophets; a Messiah and his disciples; and believers in the early church.

As they read scriptural texts, leaders are quick to see how people grieve significant losses and struggle with their capacity to attach anew. In these texts, leaders experience the movement of God's people over time, the inspiration of God's people in revelatory moments, and God's calling people into a new future.

In carefully reading God's stories, leaders increasingly see the relation of God's stories to our stories. In these connecting points, leaders may begin to discover a new vision for the congregation.

Confessional Values

Congregational leaders may find confessional values in a number of sources. A primary source across denominational traditions is Scripture itself. From Genesis to Revelation, God's values are embedded in scriptural stories. An essential task for people of faith is the interpretation of what God values and the alignment of our values to God's values.

As a minister of the Word and Sacrament in the Presbyterian Church (U.S.A.), I appreciate another source for discerning God's values: the confessional dimension of this denomination. In its confessions, the Presbyterian Church declares to its members and to the world (a) who and what it is, (b) what it believes, and (c) what it resolves to do.[2] Further, the Presbyterian Church identifies the Church of Jesus Christ as the provisional demonstration of what God intends for all of humanity, a sign of the new reality God has made available to people in Jesus Christ.[3] Presbyterian Church values are articulated as it participates in God's activity in the world by:

+ healing and reconciling and binding up wounds;
+ ministering to the needs of the poor, the sick, the lonely, and the powerless;
+ engaging in the struggle to free people from sin, fear, oppression, hunger and injustice;
+ giving itself and its substance to the service of those who suffer; and
+ sharing with Christ in the establishing of his just, peaceable, and loving rule in the world.[4]

These statements are not distinctly Presbyterian. Others may easily see their values in these statements. Whatever our tradition, we can discover in many sources what we and others have interpreted as God's values: confessional documents, books by historical and contemporary theologians, pastors' sermons, educational curricula, congregational documents, and the arrangement of sacred space in church sanctuaries.

As with God's stories and our stories, congregational leaders are wise to explore the relation of God's values to congregational values. This exploration may stimulate new vision as the congregation looks toward the future.

Illumining Prayer

As leaders seek vision in God's values and stories, they use prayer in various ways as they strive to discern the future. Sometimes prayer begins and concludes a discernment meeting. Sometimes leaders pray for clarity of direction as they consider future choices.

As leaders seek vision in God's values and stories, I suggest that they seek illumination in prayer. For some people, illumining prayer slows the process of thinking so that new thoughts may emerge in the silence. For others, illumining prayer creates sacred space in which leaders may sense the presence of God and stirrings within their imaginations.

To me, illumining prayer invites God to speak to us in the space of our silence. It acknowledges our reliance on God's presence and guidance. It reaffirms our faith that God is leading us. It opens our hearts and creates the possibility that we may find new inspiration in God's stories and values as we listen with anticipation for how our stories and values continue to form.

For Reflection and Discussion

1. What scriptural stories are most significant to your congregation? How do these stories shed light upon existing and emerging stories in your congregation?

2. From Scripture and other sources, what do you interpret as values of primary significance to God? How do these values compare to the existing and emerging values of your congregation?

3. What visions are emerging in the intersections of God's values and stories with your congregation's values and stories?

Setting a Course for the Future

One of the most creative things leaders do is to *set a course for the future*. Amid opportunities, challenges, and choices, leaders help their congregations envision new possibilities and pursue new directions. They find vision in the intersections of God's values and stories with congregational stories and values. They help congregations make connections between their identity, mission, and vision by exploring relationships between three questions:

1. Who are we? (identity)
2. Why do we exist? (mission)
3. To what do we aspire? (vision)[5]

The following examples reflect ways in which several congregations have set a course for the future by exploring visions that grow out of their identity and mission.

◆   Congregation A is a new Christian fellowship located in a rural area, thirty minutes from a midsize city. It is housed in a small multipurpose building on a large parcel of land in a county whose population is growing rapidly. Noting opportunities to develop new ministries and to grow in membership size, the congregation sees its identity as that of a new, evolving community of faithful people. Its *mission* is to share the Good News of Jesus Christ to its community and to be a living community of praise and worship. Its *vision* is to become a place for the education and formation of

Christian disciples and an outpost for mission, service, and justice in the community and world.

• Congregation B is an established Christian community that has not grown as anticipated. The congregation's lack of membership growth has resulted in a loss of enthusiasm. Its leaders believe that growth remains possible if each member participates more actively in worship and Christian education, and shares time and gifts in congregational ministries. The congregation's *mission* is to be a community of God's people empowered by the Holy Spirit to grow in grace, to celebrate God's active love in the world; to remain faithful to the path of Jesus Christ and its theological heritage; to be open to new people, ideas, and possibilities; to show compassion to individuals, the community, and the world; and to strengthen members' spiritual bonds to one another, all humanity, and God. Its *vision* is to strengthen the ministry of the people, by the people, and for the people. Underlying this vision is a commitment to five core principles:

> God has a special calling for you.
> This congregation's task is to help you find that calling.
> God has a special calling for this congregation.
> Each of us is called to help this congregation attain that calling.
> All of us, individually and corporately, are called to ministry.

• Congregation C is a large and historic church in a growing community. It has a substantial number of affluent members, and it expects excellence in each of its ministries. Its *mission* is to tell the good news of salvation by the grace of God through faith in Jesus Christ. Its *vision* is described below:

> In response to God's love for all humankind as shown in the life, death and resurrection of Jesus Christ, this congregation is called to a rich worship, a lively witness, and a

joyful welcome to all people. We will actively engage one another in stimulating, informative, supportive ministries that nurture and challenge our faith and enable us to minister in a changing community and world. We will risk opening ourselves to new understandings of our relationships with God and one another. We will share our faith, gifts, and talents with our brothers and sisters in our community and the world.

Congregational goals that express this vision are to create a growing church, ensure a vital Christian community, deepen members' relationship with God, and share their gifts with others.

Leaders in established congregations sometimes struggle to formulate a vision that captures the imagination of their members. Caught between a deep identity with a tradition and a yearning to be creative, they are prone to use formal language that speaks to the head instead of the heart. Imagine an established congregation whose leaders describe their vision in these words:

We know we are an established church. Sometimes we may be a little too predictable, but we are always here for you—in your personal transitions, in periods of joy and sorrow, in the peaks and valleys of your faith journey. We're predictably here for you.

For Reflection and Discussion

With your congregation in mind, respond to these questions:

1. Who are we?
2. Why do we exist?
3. To what do we aspire?

The Hard Work of
Setting a Course for the Future

Discovering vision in values and stories and setting a course for the future—these tasks are creative work, as well as hard work. Amid opportunities, challenges, and choices, leaders must decide which directions to pursue. While these decisions reflect congregational priorities, they will not match the priorities of each member.

As leaders set a course for the future, some members will be disappointed with its trajectory. They may say, "This is *not* the congregation I joined and have given so much to." They may become critical of leaders and staff and describe the leadership as ineffective.

When leaders feel pressure from members dissatisfied with emerging visions for the congregation, they may lose their creative energy for discovering and casting a vision. They may simplify—and neutralize—the vision, and turn toward working on goals that include the priorities of all members. They may work diligently toward these goals but without clear direction for the future. Without a sense of direction to guide them and vision to inspire their work, they will flounder.

It is easy for leaders to lose energy for the creative work of setting a course for the future. Hearing criticism, they may become discouraged. When casting a vision becomes supplanted by goal-setting exercises, they may become bogged down in details. When they sense apathy in members for the emerging vision, they may wonder, "Why bother?"

To leaders whose enthusiasm for casting a vision is waning, I offer three suggestions. First, *stay the course*. Remember that leadership is exercised against a backdrop of loss and that some people are grieving as their congregation is changing. Remember that change generates anxiety as members feel uncertain about the congregation's future. Remember that a vision is imperative if members are to attach anew.

Second, *continue to be open to other people and transparent in your communication.* Listen to members' ideas, concerns, and feelings, and communicate your care for them. Model and invite openness and honesty in conversations. Encourage people to articulate their hopes, dreams, concerns, and fears for the congregation. After all, they deeply love and are committed to the congregation, as are you.

Third, *continue to create a congregational environment in which people can deepen relationships with each other and God.* Congregations are relational entities, and healthy relationships yield healthy congregations. To be healthy, people must trust each other. Without trust, the best of visions cannot keep a congregation from floundering.

The Joy of Setting a Course for the Future

Change and loss, grieving and attaching anew. Anxiety and fear, uncertainty and hope. The past, the present, and the future. Core narratives and core values. Impediments to vision. Opportunities, challenges, and choices. The challenge to prioritize. It is easy for congregations to become overwhelmed, to flounder, and to lose their joy for ministry. In the midst of change, it is easy to lose sight of what truly defines us— namely the grace of our Lord Jesus Christ, the love of God, and the communion of the Holy Spirit (2 Cor. 13:13).

The joy of setting a course for the future ultimately comes in our remembering that our future is in God's hands. Our efforts to discover vision in values and stories and to set a course for the future are responses to the presence of God in our lives. This graceful presence invites us to follow, as with Abram . . .

> Now the Lord said to Abram, "Go from your country and your kindred and your father's house to the land that I will show you. I will make of you a great nation, and I will bless you, and make your name great, so that you will be a blessing. I will bless those who

bless you, and the one who curses you I will curse; and in you all the families of the earth shall be blessed." So Abram went, as the LORD had told him; and Lot went with him.

GENESIS 12:1–4A

. . . and the first disciples of Jesus:

As Jesus passed along the Sea of Galilee, he saw Simon and his brother Andrew casting a net into the sea—for they were fishermen. And Jesus said to them, "Follow me and I will make you fish for people." And immediately they left their nets and followed him. As he went a little farther, he saw James son of Zebedee and his brother John, who were in their boat mending the nets. Immediately he called them; and they left their father Zebedee in the boat with the hired men, and followed him.

MARK 1:16–20

These call stories invite us to experience anew the life-changing presence of God. They cast a vision of a new reality where God redeems all creation. They point toward the fulfillment of God's purposes in the world and the establishment of the reign of God.

In response, we follow in joyful anticipation of what lies ahead of us. We follow, sometimes leaving behind significant parts of our identities. We follow with confidence in the life-giving promises of God—like Abram and Sarai; like the disciples of Jesus; like other congregations that follow God and find their future.

For Reflection and Discussion

1. What excites you about setting a course for the future?
2. What concerns you?
3. What brings you the most joy as a leader?
4. Where do you go from here?

CHAPTER SIX

The Call to Lead Strategically

Will you seek to serve the people with energy, intelligence, imagination, and love?[1] This question, drawn from the *Book of Order* of the Presbyterian Church (U.S.A.), is asked in the service of ordination and installation of church officers. Elsewhere the *Book of Order* describes the purpose and pattern of leadership in the church in terms of service, after the manner of the servant ministry of Jesus Christ.[2] The call to lead is a call to serve with energy, intelligence, imagination, and love.

There is nothing uniquely Presbyterian about this question or the identification of church leadership as servant leadership. Leaders in other traditions may also find this question helpful as they think about what leadership requires.

When I hear this question asked, I find myself wondering what respondents are thinking. Some may feel relief that they have completed a time of preparation for becoming a church officer. Some may be enthusiastic as they envision leading with imagination and serving in love. Some have heard this question so many times that they are deadened to what it is asking.

+ Will you seek to serve the people with *energy*?
+ Will you seek to serve the people with *intelligence*?
+ Will you seek to serve the people with *imagination*?
+ Will you seek to serve the people with *love*?

Leadership requires much of those who accept its mantle. Those who follow leaders deserve the best that leaders can offer.

Leadership requires *energy*—physical and emotional, psychological and spiritual. The previous chapters of this book describe the challenging work of leadership. Leadership calls for active engagement and considerable amounts of energy. It requires stick-to-it-iveness and stamina, since there are no quick fixes in leadership. Leaders are wise to seek sources to renew their energy within the congregation and the community in which they serve.

Leadership demands *intelligence*: conceptual and emotional intelligence; social and contextual intelligence. Leadership demands multiple intelligences to see the opportunities, challenges, and choices before a congregation. Possessing multiple facets of intelligence increases the likelihood that leaders will respond effectively in the context of change and loss, grieving and attaching anew.

Leadership calls for *imagination*. Unfortunately, imagination is often a casualty of loss in congregations struggling with change. The pain of loss, concerns over congregational survival, and pressures to restore the status quo threaten creative ministry and leadership. Many congregations going through change want leaders who are more able to repackage the past than to visualize the future. A lively imagination in leaders expands their capacity to be energetic, intelligent, and loving. Imagine that!

Leadership requires *love*: love for the congregation, for members and other leaders, for neighbors near and far, and for God. Leaders participate in a web of caring relationships. Therefore, attention to relationships is a core function of strategic leadership. Leaders without love for each of these are less able to serve, at least in the tradition of the servant ministry of Jesus Christ. Leaders with love for each will be followed for a long time.

For Reflection and Discussion

1. Which attribute is your greatest strength as a leader: energy, intelligence, imagination, or love?
2. Which attribute do you most need to develop?
3. Where do you see the presence of these attributes in other leaders? How do their attributes strengthen your leadership?
4. Which attribute does your leadership team most need to develop?

Serving the People

Congregations are changing. In the turmoil of change, congregations need energetic, intelligent, imaginative, and loving leaders who help them with two related tasks:

+   Facing their losses.
+   Finding their future.

Some leaders excel in helping their congregation face their losses. They love the congregation for what it has been. They listen well as members share treasured memories. They grieve with those who grieve but neglect to help these members construct a future.

Other leaders are passionate about helping the congregation find its future. They love the congregation for what it may become. Seeing many opportunities for congregational growth, they may plunge ahead with great enthusiasm for change. Unfortunately, they may leave many people behind who have not prepared for change.

Strategic leaders understand that they are called to serve people through attending to their losses and helping to discern their future. Such leaders understand that both tasks are critical for congregations to find their way through changes. Key principles presented in this book include these:

1. The church both yearns for and resists effective leadership, particularly transformational leadership that is oriented to change.

2. In a time of change, many congregations look for leaders who will make their problems and challenges simple. Instead, they need leaders who will help develop their capacities to respond effectively to the challenges at hand.

3. Change challenges the adaptability, flexibility, and resilience of many congregations.

4. Some members experience change as loss.

5. Many congregations have experienced significant losses and are grieving profoundly. Their grief is shaped significantly by the depth of their attachment to those things they have lost, are losing, or fear losing.

6. These losses have resulted in a loss of energy, vitality, and passion for ministry in many congregations. Amid these losses, the needs for and expectations of effective leadership become more intense.

7. A key challenge for leaders is guiding a process through which congregations can grieve their losses and develop a capacity to *attach anew*. The capacity to attach anew is born of faith, inspired by hope, and reflected in vision.

8. Congregations without vision often flounder as they attempt to embrace change. Many congregations seeking vision face impediments that thwart their ability to cast a vision.

9. Congregations set a course for the future by finding vision in their existing and emerging values and stories, and in God's values and stories. The joy of this effort ultimately comes from remembering that the future is in God's hands.

10. Strategic leadership cannot be exercised alone. It is always offered in relation to God, congregational members and other leaders, and communities. Effective leadership is a

function of relationships. In the absence of relationships, there is not much point in leading.

A Pause to Reflect

As you reflect on the emphases of this book, how would you share your insights in a congregational newsletter? In a staff meeting? In a retreat for church leaders?

Seeking to Serve

Will you *seek to serve* the people with energy, intelligence, imagination, and love? When I reflect on this question, I recognize that the congregational leaders I will follow are seekers. They yearn to grow as leaders in response to God's calling and the needs of their congregations. They hold several convictions.

First, they believe *congregational leadership is an expression of discipleship.* They understand themselves primarily as followers who respond to God's call, presence, and empowerment. They know that faithful following and service precede effective leadership.

Second, they believe that *congregational leadership is grounded in relationships.* These leaders recognize that healthy relationships are a key to effective ministry. They realize that their effectiveness is measured by how they assist others to embrace change and move forward together.

Third, they believe that *congregational leadership is contextual.* They grasp that an effective style of leadership in one congregation will not necessarily be effective in another where histories, members, and needs are different. Leaders who comprehend the distinct qualities and needs of their current congregations are likely to serve well.

Fourth, they believe that *the behavioral sciences, leadership theories, and other secular resources contribute important perspectives for congregational leadership.* Yet they assess these perspectives through the "eyes of faith," identify their contributions and limitations, and incorporate their best practices to strengthen ministry.

Finally, they believe that *leadership is learned*. Whatever natural gifts they bring to ministry, they realize that there always is more to learn about leadership. They understand that learning to lead increases their capacity to serve.

The call to lead is before you: *Will you seek to serve the people with energy, intelligence, imagination, and love?* Will you seek to lead as they face their losses and find their future?

Notes

CHAPTER ONE

1. Ronald A. Heifetz, *Leadership Without Easy Answers* (Cambridge, Mass.: Belknap Press, 1994), 2.
2. John P. Kotter, *Leading Change* (Boston: Harvard Business School Press, 1996).
3. Ibid., 42.
4. John P. Kotter and Dan S. Cohen, *The Heart of Change: Real-Life Stories of How People Change Their Organizations* (Boston: Harvard Business School Press, 2002), 1.
5. Ibid., 17.
6. Nancy J. Barger and Linda K. Kirby, *The Challenge of Change in Organizations: Helping Employees Thrive in the New Frontier* (Palo Alto: Davies-Black Publishing, 1995), 73–76.

CHAPTER TWO

1. Ronald A. Heifetz and Marty Linsky, *Leadership on the Line: Staying Alive through the Dangers of Leadership* (Boston: Harvard Business School Press, 2002), 11.
2. Leaders who would like to explore their preferred conflict-management styles may find it helpful to work with

a conflict-management survey. Two that I have used are *Thomas-Kilmann Conflict Mode Instrument* (developed by Kenneth W. Thomas and Ralph H. Kilmann) and *Discover Your Conflict Management Style* (developed by Speed B. Leas).

3. John Bowlby, *Attachment,* vol. 1 of *Attachment and Loss,* 2nd ed. (New York: Basic Books, 1982), 207.

4. Ibid., 209.

5. Bowlby's identification and beginning discussion of these three phases may be found in *Attachment,* 27–28.

6. The discussion of these patterns of attachment is drawn from John Bowlby's last publication, *A Secure Base: Parent-Child Attachment and Healthy Human Development* (New York: Basic Books, 1988), 124–129.

7. Some contemporary attachment theorists have hypothesized a fourth pattern of attachment: *disorganized attachment.* From their perspective, this pattern results when an object of attachment is experienced simultaneously as a "safe haven" and a "source of danger." As a result, a person with an affectional bond to this object is uncertain whether to approach or to avoid the object of attachment. I find similarities between this pattern and the *anxious resistant* pattern. For further information on the pattern of *disorganized attachment,* see the description by David Wallin in *Attachment in Psychotherapy* (New York: Guilford Press, 2007), 22–23.

8. These insights are described in greater detail in three of Lee Kirkpatrick's publications: (a) "An Attachment-Theory Approach to the Psychology of Religion," *The International Journal for the Psychology of Religion* 2, no. 1 (1992): 3–28; (b) "A Longitudinal Study of Changes in Religious Belief and Behavior as a Function of Individual Differences in Adult Attachment Style," *Journal for the Scientific Study of Religion* 36, no. 2 (1997): 207–217; and (c) *Attachment,*

Evolution, and the Psychology of Religion (New York: Guilford Press, 2005).

9. John Bowlby, *The Making and Breaking of Affectional Bonds* (London: Tavistock Publications, 1979), 145–146.

CHAPTER THREE

1. John Bowlby, *Loss: Sadness and Depression*, vol. 3 of *Attachment and Loss* (New York: Basic Books, 1980), 85.

2. For further discussion of each of these variables, see *Loss*, 172–195. Although Bowlby's perspectives within these variables focus on attachments to other people, it is important to consider these variables in relation to significant attachments to places and things.

3. Elisabeth Kubler-Ross, *On Death and Dying* (New York: Macmillan, 1969).

4. Ibid., 138.

5. Wayne E. Oates, *Your Particular Grief* (Philadelphia: Westminster, 1981), 15.

6. A discussion of these areas is provided in Oates, *Your Particular Grief*, 16–21.

7. Ibid., 19.

8. Oates devotes a chapter to each of these dimensions of grief and provides relevant examples of losses, rich insights into how people experience loss, and resources for how people may move through the grieving process with each.

9. Kenneth R. Mitchell and Herbert Anderson, *All Our Losses, All Our Griefs: Resources for Pastoral Care* (Philadelphia: Westminster, 1983), 53.

10. Ibid., 54–55.

11. Ibid., 82–83.

12. Ibid., 61.

13. A discussion of these elements is provided in Mitchell and Anderson, *All Our Losses, All Our Griefs*, 62–82.

14. Ibid., 95–97.

15. Ibid., 97–100.

16. For more information on Karen Horney's work in the area of anxiety, see *Our Inner Conflicts* (New York: W.W. Norton & Company, 1945).

17. Wilfred Bion's theory of group relations is described in *Experiences in Groups, and Other Papers* (London: Tavistock Publications, 1961).

18. Readers who wish to explore these and other concepts of systems theory are referred to Edwin Friedman's *Generation to Generation: Family Process in Church and Synagogue* (New York: Guilford Press, 1985) and Peter Steinke's *Leadership in Anxious Times: Being Calm and Courageous No Matter What* (Herndon, Va.: Alban Institute, 2006).

19. Ronald Heifetz has stimulated my thinking with the metaphor of a pressure cooker for regulating levels of stress and anxiety. See *Leadership Without Easy Answers* (Cambridge, Mass.: Belknap Press, 1994), 85–86, 106, and 128.

CHAPTER FIVE

1. Richard Morrill offers a helpful discussion on the relationship of narratives to identity, mission, and vision in *Strategic Leadership: Integrating Strategy and Leadership in Colleges and Universities* (Westport, Ct.: Praeger, 2007), 142.

2. *The Constitution of the Presbyterian Church (U.S.A.), Part II: Book of Order 2007–2009* (Louisville: Office of the General Assembly, Presbyterian Church [U.S.A.]), G-2.0100a.

3. Ibid., G-3.0200a.

4. Ibid., G-3.0300c(3).

5. Morrill, *Strategic Leadership*, 142.

CHAPTER SIX

1. *The Constitution of the Presbyterian Church (U.S.A.), Part II: Book of Order 2007–2009,* W-4.4003h.
2. Ibid., G-14.0110.

For Further Reading

Burns, James MacGregor. *Transforming Leadership: A New Pursuit of Happiness*. New York: Atlantic Monthly Press, 2003.

For insights into the differences between transformational and transactional leadership, the power of vision and values in working for change, the necessary emergence of conflict as leaders make decisions, and the complex relationships between leaders and followers.

Dudley, Carl S., and Nancy T. Ammerman. *Congregations in Transition: A Guide for Analyzing, Assessing, and Adapting in Changing Communities*. San Francisco: Jossey-Bass, 2002.

For practical tools to help congregations come to grips with change, clarify a vision for ministry, and develop new habits and practices as members assimilate new patterns and perspectives.

Hamman, Jaco J. *When Steeples Cry: Leading Congregations through Loss and Change*. Cleveland: Pilgrim, 2005.

For exploring relationships between loss and grief and the ways congregational leaders facilitate mourning through formal and informal conversations, Sunday morning worship, and ministries of compassion.

Heifetz, Ronald A. *Leadership Without Easy Answers*. Cambridge, Mass.: Belknap Press, 1994.

For theoretical insights into the differences between technical and adaptive challenges, the primary functions of leadership, the relation of leadership to authority, and the inner discipline needed to stay alive as a leader.

Heifetz, Ronald A., and Marty Linsky. *Leadership on the Line: Staying Alive through the Dangers of Leadership*. Boston: Harvard Business School Press, 2002.

For practical applications of *Leadership Without Easy Answers*, with particular attention to how to manage your personal vulnerability in leading and how to sustain your spirit through tough times.

Kotter, John P., and Dan S. Cohen. *The Heart of Change: Real-Life Stories of How People Change Their Organizations*. Boston: Harvard Business School Press, 2002.

For insights into the reasons why large-scale changes either succeed or fail, eight stages of successful change, primary challenges at each stage of the process, and strategies for making changes stick.

Morrill, Richard L. *Strategic Leadership: Integrating Strategy and Leadership in Colleges and Universities*. Westport, Ct.: Praeger, 2007.

For insights into the relationships of narratives and identity, mission and vision, internal and external contexts, conflict and change, and strategic leadership and strategic management. This book is relevant to congregations.

Rendle, Gilbert R. *Leading Change in the Congregation: Spiritual and Organizational Tools for Leaders*. Bethesda, Md.: Alban Institute, 1998.

For practical guidance and tools as leaders explore the emotional processes of change, the spiritual journey of change, and the relevance of family-systems theory to changing congregations.

Rendle, Gilbert R., and Alice Mann. *Holy Conversations: Strategic Planning as a Spiritual Practice for Congregations.* Bethesda, Md.: Alban Institute, 2003.

>   For a model of congregational planning and a wealth of resources to assist congregations in resolving critical issues in strategic planning and discerning responses to three questions: Who are we? What has God called us to do or be? Who is our neighbor?

Steinke, Peter L. *Congregational Leadership in Anxious Times: Being Calm and Courageous No Matter What.* Herndon, Va.: Alban Institute, 2006.

>   For insights into how leaders respond to the effects of anxiety in their congregations, especially in handling emotional reactivity, addressing boundaries, offering clarity, and using conflict as an opportunity for learning and growth.